Ignite
CULTURE

A Train-the-Trainer Guidebook for Business Leadership

MASTERCLASS COMPANION WORKBOOK

MARGARET GRAZIANO

Distribution by Bublish
Published by KeenAlignment Press

ISBN: 978-1-647048-22-8 (paperback)

Table of Contents

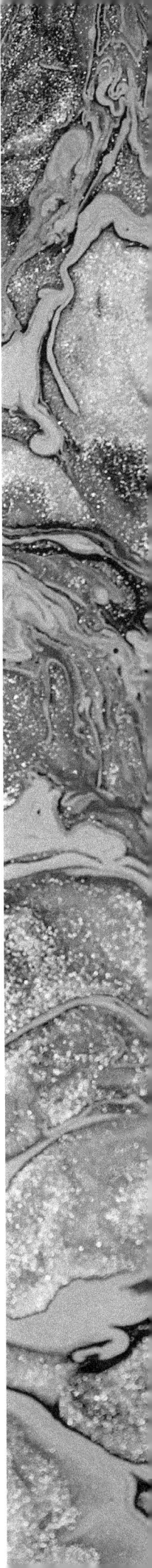

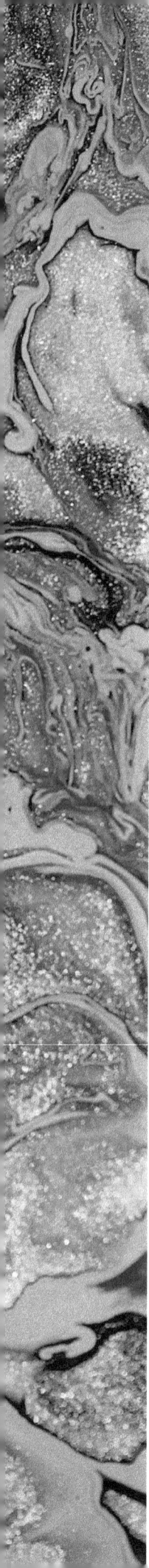

TAKE MY

ORGANIZATIONAL CULTURE

ASSESSMENT

This free tool provides specific,
tailored insights to help you analyze the current
health of your organizational culture.

Workbook Curriculum
Ignite Culture

Promise/Intention

As a result of fully engaging in this guidebook and master class suite, organizational leaders gain a comprehensive understanding of the architecture and environment required for shaping, building, and leading an emergent culture—one that anticipates, responds, and thrives in today's and tomorrow's complex business climate.

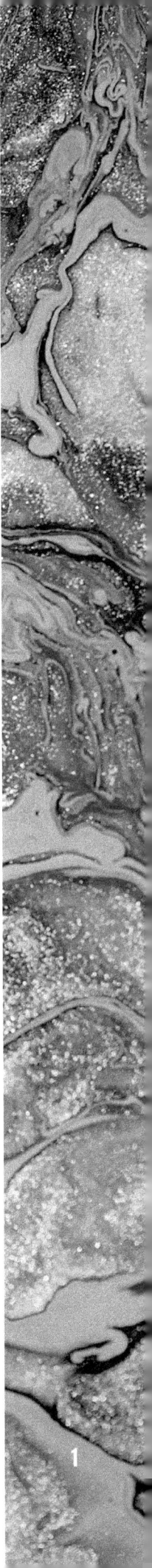

This equips learners to meet the moment by teaching the following:

- How to empower and develop yourself as a person who can effectively inspire people and lead change efforts (even and especially in the face of no agreement, resistance, and resignation).
- How to diagnose the organizational constraints by utilizing the power of unbiased, implicit, and explicit data.
- How to present organizational challenges as opportunities to innovate and lead the market.
- How to catalyze your vision, inspire partnership, and elicit contribution.
- How to set people up for a successful change journey.
- How to build a collective, a cohort, or a team of culture catalysts that work together to unlock the collective genius of an emergent culture and make real progress toward market leadership.

Audience

- CEOs, HR leaders, and members of the executive, leadership, and management teams who want to lead organizational change efforts and move toward an emergent culture with the support of powerful training and guidance.

Learning Path Objectives

- **Learn how to bring yourself up to the change challenge needing your attention.** You will learn the skills required to have the right conversations that influence the collective to contribute to change efforts. You will learn how to utilize and understand data to diagnose root causes of organizational constraints. Lastly, you will learn the formula for creating positive, high-impact, sustainable, organizational change.

- **Be aware that this is a journey, not a destination.** Lasting, positive progress requires continual intention and attention to organizational constraints, friction in workflows, and the health of the human system. Being a market leader requires individuals and the collective to adopt a growth mindset and to operate in and above the line more often than not and to be response agile.

- **Understand that you need to be operating with a conscious use of self most of the time.** This will require grit and determination, first and foremost from yourself. This journey requires you to commit to continually checking in with yourself about where you are operating from on the seven levels of effectiveness and practicing presence. It will require you to choose to be above the line and response agile. The most successful change initiatives are executed and adopted by the collective. Leading people through the challenge of change most often requires the support and guidance of a network of contribution from those who have been on this journey before and have experienced successes, failures, and lessons. We highly recommend you ask for and accept support and guidance. It is not a sign of weakness; it is a sign of commitment and courage.

- **Realize that you are empowered and equipped, and experience yourself as having what it takes to be somebody who catalyzes emergence in your organization.** You begin to know yourself and the people you enroll in rolling out change initiatives as the people who make it happen. Culture catalysts are the "intel" inside.

- **Be able to have conversations for action, build trust, and lead people to catalyze and thrive in the midst of organizational change and improvement.**

Tools/Resources

- Videos
- Brain hacks
- Checklists
- Worksheets
- Self-reflective inventory exercises
- Infographics
- Downloadable job aides
- Additional resources list
- Additional assignments

Assessments

- Short assessments are required for each section in this workbook.
- A midterm knowledge assessment is available to prepare for the final
- A final exam

Time Commitment

- One to two hours per week

For a deeper level of training take our Ignite Culture Masterclass series and catalyze culture from the inside out. https://bit.ly/4dWSVtP

Section 1

The Leader—All Change Begins with a Conscious Use of Self

Welcome and Introduction

If you are like me, you are called to make a difference. You want to bring light to others. You have a deep desire to contribute to others in a way that opens hearts and minds to the possibility of a new way of working.

This workbook gives you step-by-step lessons, inquiries and exercises that allow you to make the difference for yourself, for those you interact with and for the teams you lead.

The workbook is formulated very similarly to the *Ignite Culture* book and the Ignite Culture Masterclass. In the field of human systems, all transformation begins with the personal, then the interpersonal, then small group (the power of eight), and then the overall organization.

First the workbook supports you in examining yourself; your purpose, your values, your insights, desires, and dreams of how people work together in service of the big vision. The exercises support you in identifying your behaviors and actions that move your vision forward and constrain or even obstruct positive change from happening.

The second part of the workbook offers you exercises that support you in building alignment with those you count on most to bring the vision to life. You are encouraged to share the personal development you have participated in and give those same tools to the five to eight people you spend the most time with.

The third section of the workbook gives you lessons and instructions about how to impact the greater whole. The power of "culture" is that it IS the result of the collection of behaviors, interactions, and actions in the whole.

Culture IS how people feel about themselves and others in the collective. It's how the collective responds or reacts to challenges, change, uncertainty, stress, chaos, and ambiguity.

Thank you so much for trusting me and for engaging in this deep and powerful inquiry of being the change you want to see.

If you would like to take the *Ignite Culture* masterclass, visit MargaretGraziano.com

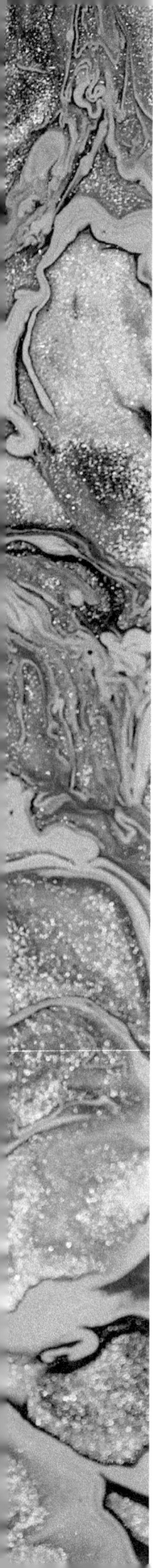

Chapter 1

Dysfunction Is Destroying Lives and Companies

Remember the cautionary tale of Volkswagen from chapter 1 of *Ignite Culture*? The company was charged with deliberately falsifying emissions tests for their diesel cars. The company's stock plummeted, its reputation was scarred, and the scandal cost Volkswagen tens of billions of euros. It was the CEO, Martin Winterkorn, who was charged with lying to the German parliament. Cultural dysfunction always starts or ends with the leadership team.

You can't just put a bandage on a culture that is broken. You have to heal these human systems to be able to move forward. In this section, you're going to get an overview of culture to better understand its impact. We're going to look at where your organization might be constrained. We'll do an analysis and inventory of those constraints by looking at the questions below.

The biggest thing we're trying to address in this section is whether dysfunction is constraining your company and the happiness, creativity, and productivity of the people within it.

So, where are you?

Is your organization showing the symptoms of a transactional, entangled, or toxic culture, where teamwork, communication, trust, and innovation are sorely lacking? Some signs of these types of cultures include perfectionism, favoritism, minimal agreement, toxicity, out-of-control egos, nitpicking, infighting, blaming, shaming, competition, powering up over others, complacency and status quo, avoidance of challenging conversations, etc. These are the very behaviors that constrain what is possible and cause systemic workplace dysfunction.

Below are some questions I recommend you review and answer in this companion workbook.

- Are you experiencing growth at the level you want to?
- Is innovation happening at the cadence and speed you want it to?
- What's happening with recruiting and retention?
- Is your noble cause compelling enough to get your people amped up and excited about their contribution?
- Is your company achieving its goals and objectives?
- Are initiatives launched and fulfilled at the rate you have said is important?
- How effective is decision-making? Is decision-making cascading down-stream or is the executive team making decisions and solving problems that really would be much better solved by the front lines or by the people who live with the problems?
- Are your meetings effective or do they often feel like wasted time?
- What is your reputation in the marketplace?
- What levels of friction are your people experiencing when trying to get work done, both interdepartmentally and intra-departmentally?
- How well does the organization adapt to change? Is change met with resistance and fear, or with a spirit of "hell yeah, we're ready to do this"?
- What do new people say when they come into the organization? How does it feel there?

How Emergent, Innovative, and Responsive Is Your Culture?

Culture is the foundation of any organization, and it starts from within. The goal is to create an emergent culture where people give discretionary effort, give new ideas, and step in where and when needed to make things better. The three components of an emergent culture are:

1. Intent – The overarching reason or noble cause the organization is committed to.

2. Environment – How people relate and work with one another, their communication, and their level of trust. The environment is how it feels to work in the organization.

3. Architecture – The structure and systems in place that create the space and energy for healthy, intentional, high-performance actions to occur. Architecture includes structures such as how planning is done, how meetings are run, new hire onboarding, and succession planning, etc.

Successful emergent cultures are the result of shared causes, missions, visions, values, and behaviors that create, shape, and foster a positive and productive work environment that is ready and adaptable to change. Remember, this is not just posting values on the wall; it's living the behaviors, being intentional, and realizing how each of these components integrates and impacts the overall culture.

This section includes an assessment with a checklist to rate your organization on a scale of one to ten, with an emergent culture being the ideal state. We'll obviously look a lot at company culture as we progress. With this assessment, you get deeper insights into what you need to know as you move forward and specifically where to focus your efforts. So, let's take a look at your current company culture, because awareness is the first step.

Checklist Inventory

On a scale of one to ten, where is your organization regarding the following questions?

Is your organization emergent enough to compete and thrive in today's and tomorrow's world? Is employee morale a help or a hindrance?

Rate the overall health of your human system (how people work, relate, solve problems, and achieve together).

Where and how is friction between processes or people negatively impacting forward momentum?

How effective are conversations for action?

List out areas in the organization that are working really well.

Next list areas that are not working well or not as well as they could.

Are you experiencing growth where you want to?

Where is the organization experiencing growth? Where is the organization stagnating?

What about your Noble Cause gets your team fired up and inspired to serve?

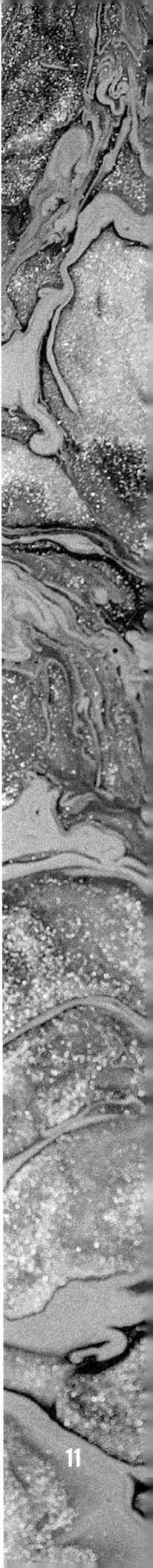

What specifically is your organization doing to encourage innovation?

What percentage of employees are achieving performance metrics? Why do you think it is this way?

How do you launch new initiates into the human system? What is the process?

How quickly is your organization moving change forward?

How's the decision-making? Are decisions being made in the spirit of who is closest to solving the problem? Or is the exec team making decisions and solving problems that would be better solved by the people closer to them?

Are meetings perceived as effective or a waste of time? Describe why you answered this way.

What is the level of friction your people experience while getting work done? What is the impact of this friction on organizational performance and employee engagement?

How well does the organization adapt to change? Is change met with resistance and fear or a "hell yeah, let's do this!" attitude?

What do new people say when they come into the organization? How does it feel there?

Would you rate your organization as an emergent culture where people are initiating and owning new ideas to make things more efficient and easier for people? If it is not emergent then is it more transactional in nature (people doing the bare minimum to get by) or entangled, where a portion of the group is defensive aggressive and another portion is passive defensive? The questions below can help illustrate these points.

Survey on How Innovation Ready Your Organization Is

These questions evaluate inclusion effectiveness and innovation readiness.

Please rate the following questions on a scale from 1 to 10, with 10 being the highest and 1 being the lowest. Write your answer in the blank provided.

At the end of your meetings or projects, how often do you specifically assess the level of engagement among participants?

Rate from 1-10: _____

At the start of your meetings or project launches, how often do you take time for all attendees to generate a common purpose for their participation together?

Rate from 1-10: _____

On average, in your meetings or work sessions, what percentage of the time is spent listening to presentations?

Rate from 1-10: _____

When launching projects, holding meetings, or facilitating innovation sessions, how many different methods of interaction do you use to engage every attendee and improve the effectiveness of the working group?

Rate from 1-10: _____

In the agendas of your meetings or work sessions, how often do you specify the method of interaction that will be used for each topic and its purpose?

Rate from 1-10: _____

In your meetings or work sessions, how often is someone acting as the facilitator?

Rate from 1-10: _____

In your meetings or work sessions, how often do you change the configuration of the group, such as from working together as a whole group, to working in small groups, pairs or individually?

Rate from 1-10: _____

In your meetings or work sessions, how often does the role of facilitator shift among members of the group?

Rate from 1-10: _____

How often do you make an intentional decision to include new people with different perspectives or functional roles in your meetings, project launches, or work sessions?

Rate from 1-10: _____

How often do you make the decision to include in your meetings or work sessions all or most of the people who will be affected by the decisions that will be made?

Rate from 1-10: _____

With your working group, how frequently do you engage as a group without presentations and with the freedom to cocreate the agenda together?

Rate from 1-10: _____

How frequently do you create opportunities for everyone to share their own ideas for moving forward without regard to formal position or rank?

Rate from 1-10: _____

How often do you deviate from your agenda to engage group members in unscripted sessions formed to respond adaptively to themes that emerged in the moment?

Rate from 1-10: _____

How frequently do you create opportunities to innovate with diverse people from other functions or with the clients you serve?

Rate from 1-10: _____

How frequently do you work together in a space that makes it possible and easy to creatively mix and reconfigure participant groups?

Rate from 1-10: _____

What is your score? _____

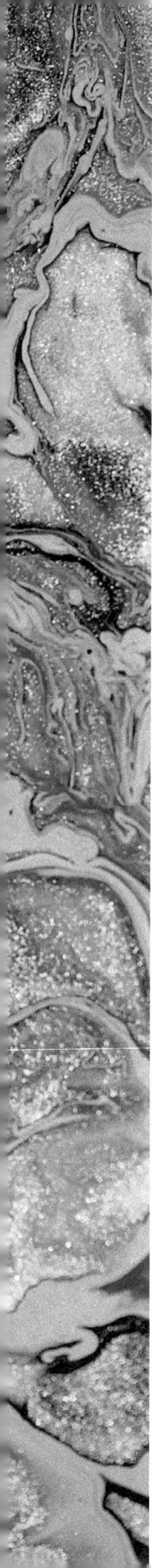

Chapter 2
Time for a Hard Look in the Mirror

Are you ready to take a hard look in the mirror? Chapter 2 is really about how you as a leader respond when things are not going your way (when you are under stress, facing large amounts of pressure, failing or feel like you're failing, and when people make big and small mistakes). It's about your personality, ego, competency, and capacity. Building a high-performance organizational culture isn't easy; it requires honesty and self-awareness.

In this section, we'll help you look at when you are *hot* and when you are *not*. You'll be introduced to the Johari window, where you'll see the axes of "what is known to self" versus "what is known to others" and see how blind spots show up in the quadrant intersecting "known to others" and "not known to self."

The Johari Window

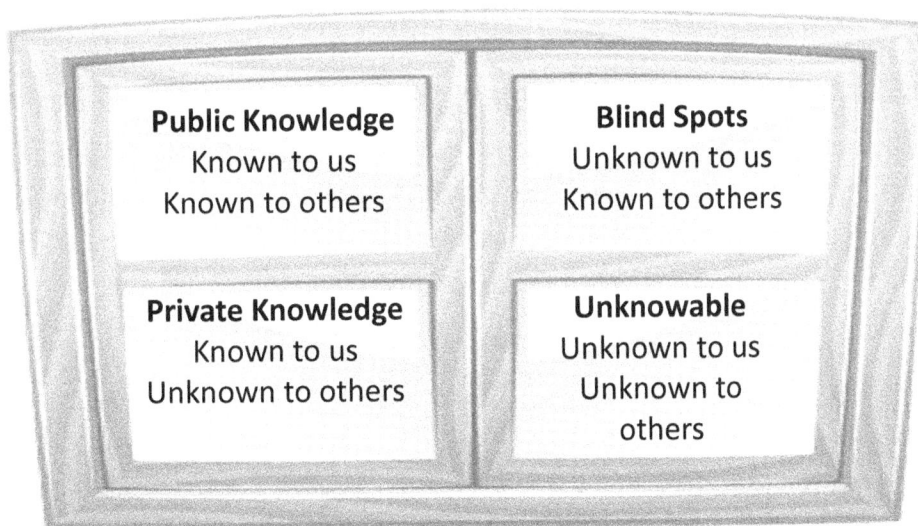

Public Knowledge
Known to us
Known to others

Blind Spots
Unknown to us
Known to others

Private Knowledge
Known to us
Unknown to others

Unknowable
Unknown to us
Unknown to others

A perfect example of this blind spot is a leader I worked with who, even after *years* of being told about the toxicity of one of his executive team members, refused to acknowledge or deal with it. For three years, the executive team had been telling him there was a member of the team who was a complete and utter jerk. He was manipulative and cruel, and he pitted people against each other. Yet the CEO was unwilling to hear it because the person (let's call him Ray) was such a high producer, and he believed the company's success was because of Ray. So, the leader turned a blind eye. The toxicity Ray was bringing to the culture was clearly "known to others," but this leader refused to let it become "known to himself." It remained a blind spot.

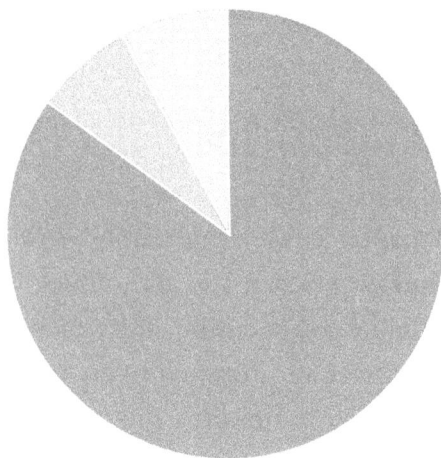

What we know we know
What we know we don't know
What we don't know we don't know

So, where are you unwilling or unable to see what's really going on? What unworkable situations have you ignored, tolerated, or stepped over? Which of your beliefs need to be updated for the emergent culture you seek?

Marshall Goldsmith, author of *What Got You Here Won't Get You There*, has said, "If you don't change your beliefs about yourself, it can be hard to change your behavior." But, if you're willing to do the work, you can override your brain's autopilot and change your behaviors. This is a skill that's necessary to fully develop the capacity to build trust, inspire people, and create positive change. You can't just say, "I'm engaged." You have to *be* engaged and willing to look at your part and your responsibility in any success or failure. You can't just overlook any toxicity that is brought into the culture, even if there is some success. As the leader, you have to look at where you are part of the problem. You'll need to discover where you have blind spots, and it's not easy due to the very nature of blind spots. Everybody has them, and you'll need to face some of yours.

The health of your organization's culture starts with you. This is your wake-up call to start looking at problems from the inside out. This exploration starts with you and your unique power and potential. Self-awareness is not something you can just visit once a year; it's an essential personal competency required if you want to effect positive change.

To do that you are invited to take a personal inventory to uncover your own blind spots and where you may be unwilling or unable to see what's going on. There will be a lot of self-discovery. Then, you'll do a visualization exercise about what you want to experience in your culture. After we walk you through the visualization of what you *want* to experience, you'll be able to see more clearly where you need to grow to be able to experience that. This will bring you to the conflicts closest to you in the business to see if you are willing to take 100-percent responsibility for them. You first have to be willing to take responsibility. Then, if you *are* willing to take 100-percent responsibility, you'll need to look at where or in what way you are responsible for those conflicts. You're the only one who can determine how you can be the contribution you really want to be.

Cultural transformation always starts with the top leadership. Organizational change isn't possible without your commitment and leadership. It's ultimately you who can set the stage. It is how you work, when you work, how you handle disappointments, how you deal with performance, and the level of transparency with which you lead.

As a leader, understanding and shaping the organizational culture is crucial for achieving the organization's goals and objectives. By creating a positive culture, leaders can promote a healthy and high-performance organization from the inside out. It starts with you. We're here to get you and your organization to the next level and to build and develop an emergent culture. So, are you ready to take that hard look in the mirror?

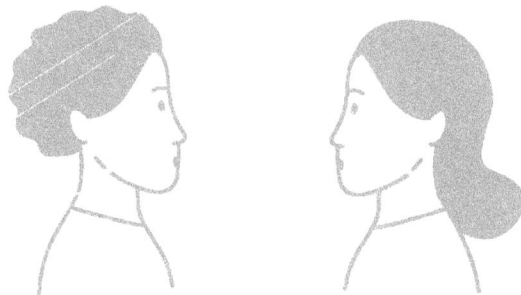

What works about you as a leader (internal)?

What works about you as a leader (external)?

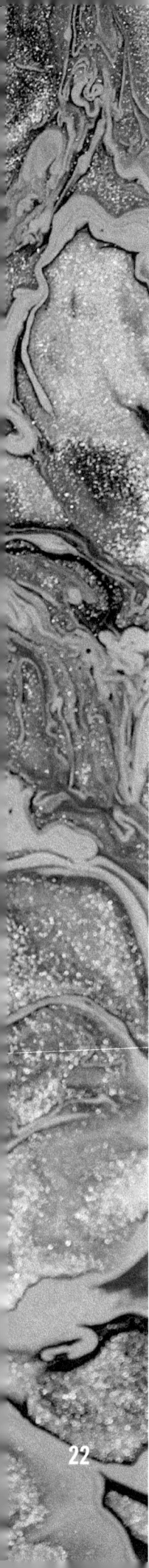

What does not work about you as a leader? What gets in your way and derails or thwarts your effectiveness (internal)?

What does not work about you as a leader? What gets in your way and derails or thwarts your effectiveness (external)?

Self-awareness is defined as the ability to know oneself and be conscious of how others see us. Psychologists separate self-awareness into two categories: internal and external. Internal self-awareness is about knowing ourselves and being conscious of our likes, our dislikes, our ambitions, our place in the environment, and our impact on other people. External self-awareness has to do with understanding how other people see us. It's about being able to look at ourselves from an outside perspective.

Internal Self-awareness	External Self-awareness
What makes me happy?	How do I show up around others?
What upsets me?	What do other people see as my strengths?
When do I get triggered?	What do other people see as my weaknesses?
What are my strengths?	What do other people think works about my leadership?
What are my weaknesses?	What do other people think doesn't work about my leadership?
What am I good at?	What do my friends and family often point out about me?
What am I so-so at?	What compliments do they give me?
What am I bad at?	What feedback do they give me?
What makes me tired?	What personality traits do they like to highlight about me?
What is the most important thing in my life?	How would other people describe me?

What stresses me out?	What is something other people say I need to work on?
What relaxes me?	How do I come across to other people?
What's my definition of success?	
What type of worker am I?	
How do I want others to see me?	
What makes me angry?	
What type of person do I want to be?	
What do I think about myself?	
What things do I value in life?	

What do you see: a rabbit or a duck?

More than one hundred years after it was first sketched, this drawing has sparked a huge reaction after being shared on social media. Some see a rabbit and others see a duck—but are you able to see both alternatively? What you see (and how fast you see it) could indicate how quickly your brain works—and how creative you are.

The duck-rabbit drawing was first used by American psychologist Joseph Jastrow in 1899 to make the point that perception is not only what one sees but also a mental activity.

From *The Independent*

"The first principle is that you must not fool yourself—
and you are the easiest person to fool."

Nobel Prize–winning physicist Richard Feynman

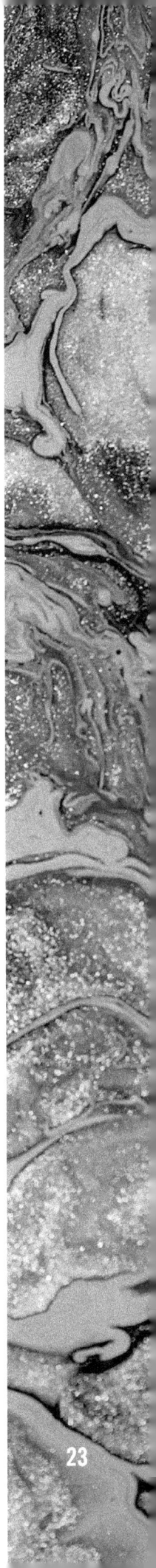

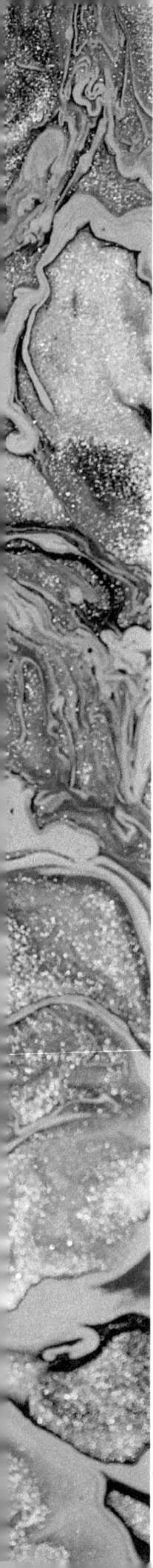

Chapter 3
Wake Up and Meet Your Higher Self

It's time to wake up and meet your higher self. Whereas the last section was more about self-awareness and seeing what's around you, in chapter 3, you'll delve deeper into who you are and explore your intrinsic motivations and why you do what you do.

The concept of the higher self is the pinnacle of Maslow's hierarchy of needs, which has five levels. The lowest level contains physiological human needs such as air, food, and water. That level is followed by safety, then belonging, and then esteem. The fifth and highest level is self-actualization, which is the complete realization of one's full potential. Achieving this is so difficult that less than 1 percent of adults ever do it. The higher self is this self-actualized version of who you were meant to be. Knowing your higher self, or at least striving to, is about understanding what life really means to you.

This section is all about who you are, your highest purpose, and your personal values—not for your career, but for yourself. What likely brought you to this workbook is that you are in a time of challenge. Maybe you're feeling stuck. Before you can bring your higher self to work, you need to face your fears and the behaviors created by your defensive, reactive mind. You need to manage your ego. If you are stuck because of your need to find blame or to be right, if you struggle with feedback and never feel satisfied, or if your relationships are strained because you ask for too much while giving too little, your ego is likely in charge, not your higher self. An organization run by the egos of its leaders struggles with growth and innovation because everyone is afraid to engage with their boss's ego.

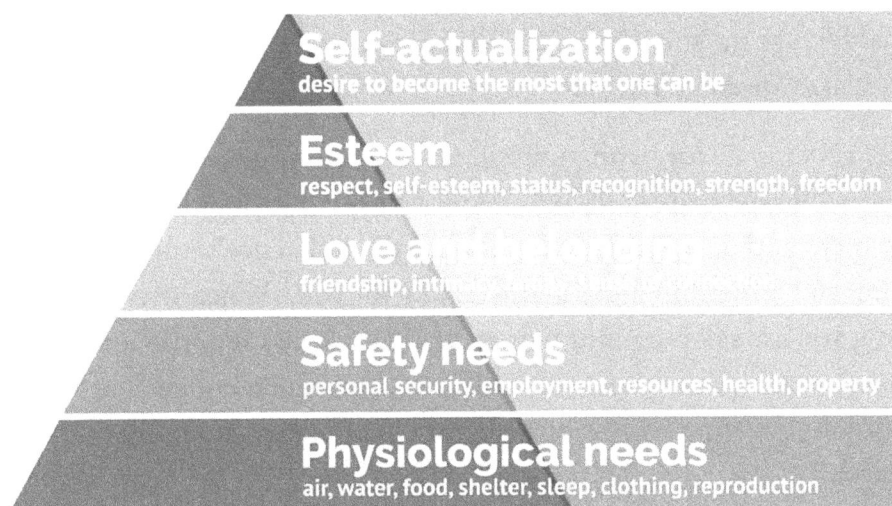

Self-actualization
desire to become the most that one can be

Esteem
respect, self-esteem, status, recognition, strength, freedom

Love and belonging
friendship, intimacy, family, sense of connection

Safety needs
personal security, employment, resources, health, property

Physiological needs
air, water, food, shelter, sleep, clothing, reproduction

Maslow's Heirarchy of Needs
https://www.simplypsychology.org/maslow.html

Your ego may be keeping you from the very exploration that could lead to better self-awareness. It's all based in fear. Even people who are very self-aware sometimes find themselves in the dark regarding their thoughts or actions. But you can't be a roadblock to your own growth. You need to be proactive instead of reactive, especially the face of a crisis. You need to find the courage to trust your abilities and create a collaborative space where self-actualization isn't just possible, but highly probable.

To that end, we'll guide you through a minivisualization of your future self and your key values. This meditation will allow you to see things through your higher self and ask powerful questions such as the following:

- Why do you do what you do?
- If it's not about the money, what is important to you?
- What are your highest values?
- Are you living your values?
- What's life really about to you?
- What is your highest purpose?

Just imagine an organizational culture led by a leader who is self-actualized and who has attained their highest capability for inspiring and encouraging people. An organization like that would be able to perform at the highest levels and allow its people to self-actualize as well. Think of the pure potential of a human system in which the work environment and culture actually encourage people to self-actualize. The possibilities are endless.

It's important to understand yourself before you can successfully lead others. This work in self-awareness and understanding of your personal values must come first, so take some time to delve into your personal values through a values worksheet. This foundational work has the power to change not just your personal life but also your professional life. It's the foundation for all that you will do. Having your values define your work makes all the difference.

If you don't get crystal clear with yourself, not only do you lose, but your organization does too. Once you are clear about your values we invite you to write a personal vision statement and document it. It makes all the difference to understand what successful living and leadership looks and feels like for you. When you get out of bed in the morning you are stepping into that articulated vision every day and you bring that sense of purpose and passion to work with you. That modeling gives others the sense that they can do the same. This is how alignment of people and purpose happens in the workplace.

You'll finish this section with a better understanding of your intrinsic motivations and how to align your life with them. These exercises give you access and clarity to your higher purpose and inspiring values. Once you have that clarity, aligning your actions, behaviors and interactions is much easier and much more rewarding. So, get ready to meet your higher self and explore your deepest motivations. This is something only you can do for yourself and your organization. Imagine the amazing culture and energy that you, your executive team, and your people could create if you all went on this journey. The upside is tremendous. Let's dive in!

Notes from the Meditation on Future Self (meditation in master class)

Exploring Your Purpose, Calling, and Ultimate Intent

The 5 elements of a calling as explored through the "Autonomy Course"

1. It's real for you. It's grounded in your own direct, personal experience.

2. It creates a world.

3. You are the source of it. . . and it's not limited to you.

4. It's what you are saying is the most important thing in your life (the ultimate concern).

5. It's actionable in any moment and circumstance.

The way to express your calling is:

People [verb] an experience that inspires you.

Identifying Personal Values

Method

Make a list of the personal qualities and values you most resonate with and specific ways you can incorporate them into your life.

Long Version

The word *values* has many definitions, but in this case it means personal qualities and ways of living that you believe in and resonate with. Psychologist Steven Hayes describes values as "chosen life directions" that are "vitalizing, uplifting, and empowering." A value is not merely a goal but can be thought of as a continuous process, direction, and way of living that helps direct us toward various goals and live a meaningful life.

Identifying Your Values

There are various ways to identify your personal values, including choosing which domains or areas in your life are most important to you and identifying what you value within each domain specifically. The areas of your life and how many you choose can vary. They can include relationships, work/career achievement, parenting, self-care (health, leisure, etc.), spirituality, community involvement, and education/learning.

Values Exercise

1. *Determine your core values.* From the list below, choose and write down every core value that resonates with you. Do not overthink your selections. As you read through the list, simply circle the words that feel like a core value to you personally. If you think of a value you possess that is not on the list, be sure to write it down as well.

Abundance	Daring	Intuition	Preparedness
Acceptance	Decisiveness	Joy	Proactivity
Accountability	Dedication	Kindness	Professionalism
Achievement	Dependability	Knowledge	Punctuality
Advancement	Diversity	Leadership	Recognition
Adventure	Empathy	Learning	Relationships
Advocacy	Encouragement	Love	Reliability
Ambition	Enthusiasm	Loyalty	Resilience
Appreciation	Ethics	Making a Difference	Resourcefulness
Attractiveness	Excellence	Mindfulness	Responsibility
Autonomy	Expressiveness	Motivation	Responsiveness
Balance	Fairness	Optimism	Security
Being the Best	Family	Open-Mindedness	Self-Control
Benevolence	Friendships	Originality	Selflessness
Boldness	Flexibility	Passion	Simplicity
Brilliance	Freedom	Performance	Stability
Calmness	Fun	Personal Development	Success
Caring	Generosity	Proactive	Teamwork
Challenge	Grace	Professionalism	Thankfulness
Charity	Growth	Quality	Thoughtfulness
Cheerfulness	Flexibility	Recognition	Traditionalism
Cleverness	Happiness	Risk-Taking	Trustworthiness
Community	Health	Safety	Understanding
Commitment	Honesty	Security	Uniqueness
Compassion	Humility	Service	Usefulness
Cooperation	Humor	Spirituality	Versatility
Collaboration	Inclusiveness	Stability	Vision
Consistency	Independence	Peace	Warmth
Contribution	Individuality	Perfection	Wealth
Creativity	Innovation	Playfulness	Well-Being
Credibility	Inspiration	Popularity	Wisdom
Curiosity	Intelligence	Power	Zeal

2. *From the list of values you just created, group all similar values together.* Group them in a way that makes sense to you personally. Create a maximum of five groupings. If you have more than five groupings, drop those least important to you. See the example below.

Abundance	Acceptance	Appreciation	Balance	Cheerfulness
Growth	Compassion	Encouragement	Health	Fun
Wealth	Inclusiveness	Thankfulness	Personal Development	Happiness
Security	Intuition	Thoughtfulness	Spirituality	Humor
Freedom	Kindness Love	Mindfulness	Well-being	Inspiration
Independence	Making a Difference			Joy
Flexibility	Open-Mindedness			Optimism
Peace	Trustworthiness			Playfulness
	Relationships			

3. *Choose one word within each grouping that best represents the label for the entire group.* Again, do not overthink your labels. There are no right or wrong answers. You are defining the answer that is right for you. See the example below—the label chosen for the grouping is in boldface.

Abundance	Acceptance	Appreciation	Balance	Cheerfulness
Growth	Compassion	Encouragement	Health	Fun
Wealth	Inclusiveness	Thankfulness	Personal Development	**Happiness**
Security	Intuition	Thoughtfulness	Spirituality	Humor
Freedom	Kindness Love	**Mindfulness**	**Well-being**	Inspiration
Independence	**Making a Difference**			Joy
Flexibility	Open-Mindedness			Optimism
Peace	Trustworthiness			Playfulness
	Relationships			

- Begin by taking some time to reflect deeply on what areas of your life and ways of living give you the most meaning, interest, and sense of fulfillment.

- Feel free to use any of the areas listed or think of your own.

- After you have chosen a few areas, evaluate how important each one is to you and rank them accordingly.

- Next, closely and honestly examine how present this value is in your current life, including daily activities, lifestyle, and relationships.

- Make note of any values that are highly ranked but not highly present in your life.

- Begin to brainstorm and list any concrete ways that you can make this value more prevalent in your life. These do not need to be major life changes but can be small actions or activities. For example, if you value spending time with your family, perhaps make an effort to have family dinner together more times each week or read a bedtime story to your children more often.

- Continue to think of different ways to further incorporate your values into your life and test them out, noting what works and, most importantly, enjoying the exploration!

History

Identifying and incorporating personal values into one's life is a long-standing tradition emphasized in many cultures and religions. The practice specifically described here was adapted from the work of leading clinical psychologists Steven Hayes, Susan Orsillo, and Lizabeth Roemer.

Cautions

Realizing that we are not truly living the life we want to live or embodying what we value can be difficult and even painful. Please remember that maintaining a compassionate and gentle approach to yourself and your discoveries is critical to the process and to creating real change.

From MindfulnessExercises.com

Chapter 4
Your People Need You in the Room

*"Always hold fast to the present. Every situation,
indeed, every moment, is of infinite value, for it
is the representative of a whole eternity."*

Johann Wolfgang von Goethe

Are you fully present? Or are you thinking about, or even doing, other things right now? Most of us aren't fully present, thanks mostly to adrenaline bias and cognitive bias. In this chapter, you'll learn ways to be more present and grounded and how that can positively affect your productivity and decision-making. You'll be able to show up with curiosity and really be in the room for your people. We want you to harness the power of presence. There's real power in that, and your people need you to be in the room.

There is so much noise coming into your brain every day. You have between twelve and sixty thousand thoughts per day, and 80–85 percent of them are negative and repetitive. And you are not alone; your employees do too. The trouble comes as you start to work for that rush of adrenaline, driving to perform through all the noise. This adrenaline bias leaves you trying to handle multiple tasks at the same time. And then, your cognitive bias has you creating mental shortcuts and filtering, which can leave critical information out of your decision-making and processing. Your body might be in the room physically, but your mind is scattered among all your tasks, and your perceptions may not be accurate. It's a big problem. One of the most important things to understand is that multitasking is a myth. Your brain is wired to focus on one thing at a time, and cognitive scattering, which happens when we jump from the right hemisphere of our brain to the left hemisphere and back again, only leads to burnout and poor decision-making. In fact, it costs organizations billions of dollars in lost time, errors, reduced creativity, and burnout. Focusing on being fully present will make a world of difference to you.

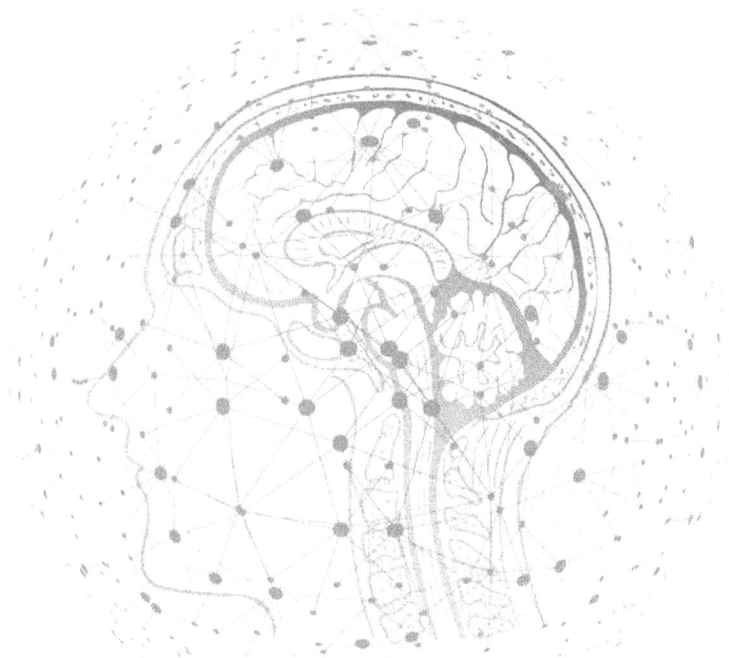

12,000 - 60,000 thoughts a day
85% negative & repetitive

It is also crucial to your growth and development that you become more and more aware of where you are on the 7 levels of effectiveness, and to notice when you are reacting instead of responding. When you're reactive, you're like a human animal, focused only on protecting and defending yourself, which almost always leads to bad behavior with systemic implications affecting the culture and the people in it. To create a high-performance organization, practicing presence allows you to operate in your highest use of self more of the time.

There are seven levels of effectiveness to consider:

1. Hopelessness - feeling stuck, despair, resignation

2. Fear - anxiety, craving, protection.

3. Frustration - annoyance, agitation, fighting against others.

4. Courage - commitment to a positive future, willingness to step forward.

5. Engagement - fully committed, desire to bring value

6. Innovation - eager to contribute to solve the perceived unsolvable.

7. Synchronicity - the realm of everything is happening for me.

* Graph available on page 111

At the lower levels of effectiveness, you're operating in ego mode and your body is flooded with brain chemicals like adrenaline, cortisol, and norepinephrine, putting you in a state of fight, flight, or freeze. In these states, you can only be happy and productive up to 25 percent of the time, and that's if you're operating in anger and frustration. That's two hours of actual work in an eight-hour day. What's worse is that in the fear level, it drops to only 10 percent, and in the hopelessness level, it's a mere 5 percent. Understanding this, you can see why being grounded, present, and responsive leads to better decision-making and increased productivity. Through presence, you get more done with your time.

A **reflection**, we learn, is a situation, event, phrase, image, or any such external (or sometimes internal) input that triggers a state of upset and emotional distress. Those situations are set up by our own actions, words, thoughts, and choices either directly (i.e., saying certain keywords or phrases to a person we know, which leads them toward the same pattern/conflict scenario we have gone through time and again) or indirectly (i.e., heading to a part of town where we subconsciously know we will meet our trigger). This is a *voluntary* process guided by our subconscious/inner self (presence) in hopes we can use the situation to resolve the open loop of some unintegrated childhood emotional trauma. (Think of a computer constantly returning to an unresolved equation and trying to process it again.)

A **projection** is the mental and physical defensive reaction to a reflection to try and defend the conscious self from the perceived emotional harm/pain. This knee-jerk reaction includes but is not limited to the inner story we tell ourselves (i.e., *He said that because he hates me*), the vocal expression (i.e., yelling or cursing toward the triggering element), the physical expression (i.e., breaking things, throwing things), and everything in between. This is a *misguided* process guided by our mental, physical and emotional body that runs counter to the reflection process, which mistakenly thinks the childhood emotional pain we are re-experiencing is *new* pain. (Think of how a body might mistake peanuts for something poisonous and trigger an allergic reaction.) In short, to *project* on a *reflection* is to shoot the messenger.

From *The Presence Process* by Michael Brown

To learn to be present, we offer a mini-meditation in our Ignite Culture Master Class, on how to get grounded. This is an exercise of mindfulness and awareness that enables you to be more present, curious, aware, and able to connect. Once you can reliability get yourself grounded and master these techniques, it will support you to approach situations with more curiosity and openness, allowing you to receive more information and thus make better decisions.

Another method for improving your ability to be and stay present is to elevate how you listen. Remember from chapter 4 that there are five levels of listening: ignoring, pretending, selective, attentive, and active or empathetic listening. It is only through active listening that the listener is fully engaged and present for the communication. Through the 7/38/55 Rule, we know that 55 percent of communication shows up in body language, 38 percent in tonality, and only 7 percent in the words we say. The earlier levels of listening are focused only on words, if they're focused at all. Body language is critical in communication, and being fully present to read body language and facial expressions supports you in being a better active and empathetic listener.

To practice these techniques, we'll be providing exercises and prompts for conversations with others. You can train people to be present, but it starts with you. By practicing being present and engaged in your interactions, you can build a more productive and healthy work culture. You will be able to harness the power of presence and use it to benefit you and your organization. So, let's get started!

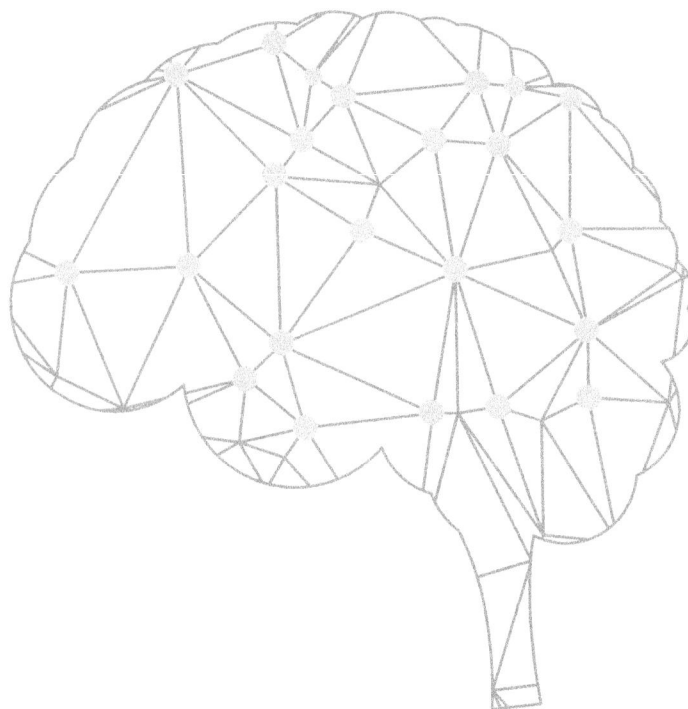

Sensory Acuity

In a general context, *sensory acuity* means how good or bad your senses are at doing what they should do. In the context of neuro-linguistic programming (NLP), it refers to the ability to use our senses to make accurate observations about ourselves and other people.

NLP sensory acuity exercise:

1. One becomes an observer, and the other becomes the subject.

2. The subject thinks of the event he/she dislikes the most.

3. Subject pays close attention to internal feelings as he/she thinks about the event.

4. Observer observes the change in physiology and other changes in the subject.

5. Then switch roles.

The Emotional Vibration Analysis Frequency Chart

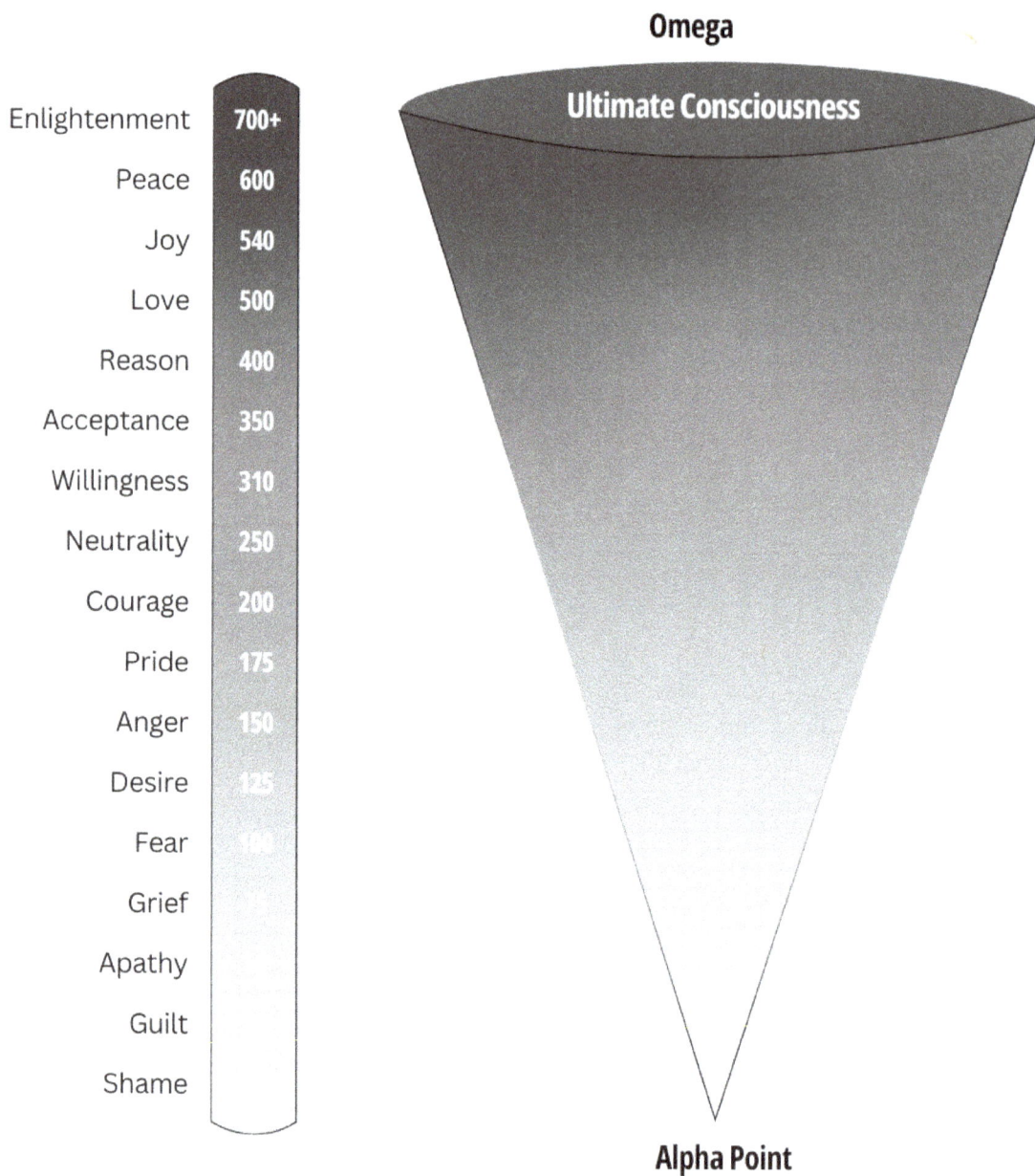

Omega

Ultimate Consciousness

Emotion	Value
Enlightenment	700+
Peace	600
Joy	540
Love	500
Reason	400
Acceptance	350
Willingness	310
Neutrality	250
Courage	200
Pride	175
Anger	150
Desire	125
Fear	100
Grief	
Apathy	
Guilt	
Shame	

Alpha Point

Consciousness Mapped

Joy is one of the highest states of consciousness on Dave Hawkins' scale, with a vibrational energy of 540. It is associated with feelings of contentment, satisfaction, and happiness that come from within rather than those that are dependent on external circumstances.

The Adrenaline Bias:

So many leaders have become accustomed to the daily rush of solving problems and managing crises that they unintentionally have become addicted to the adrenaline high, which quite often leads to destructive behavior and unhealthy work culture.

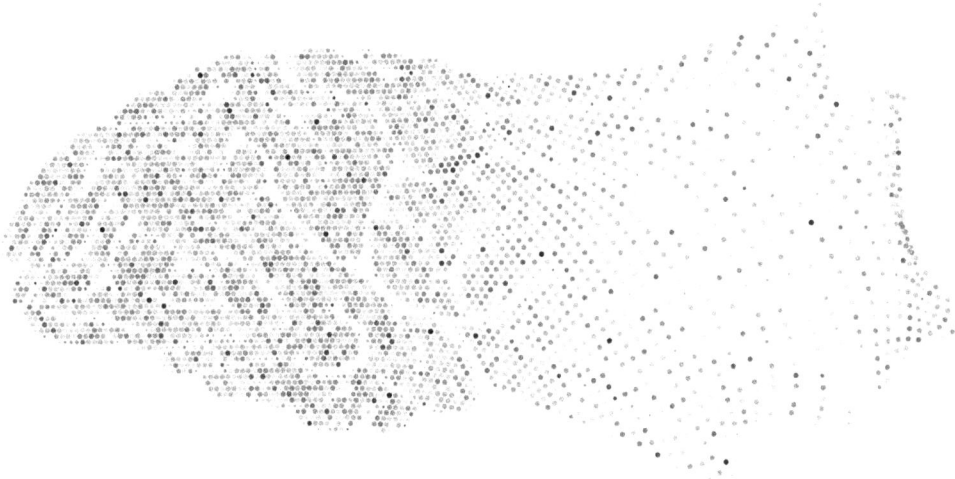

Questions to think and journal about:

How stressed are you?

What are the things distracting you?

Where is an adrenaline bias getting in your way?

What are your triggers (what takes you off track)?

In what areas are you doing well? What areas need further development? Rank them from one to ten.

We invite you to check out The KeenAlignment Learning Center "Brain Hacks" which will support you in deepening your learning and forwarding your mastery.

https://www.keenalignment.com/post/the-importance-of-slowing-down

Notes on Presence Exercise Meditation

Check out the brain hack on page 54 of the *Ignite Culture Book*.

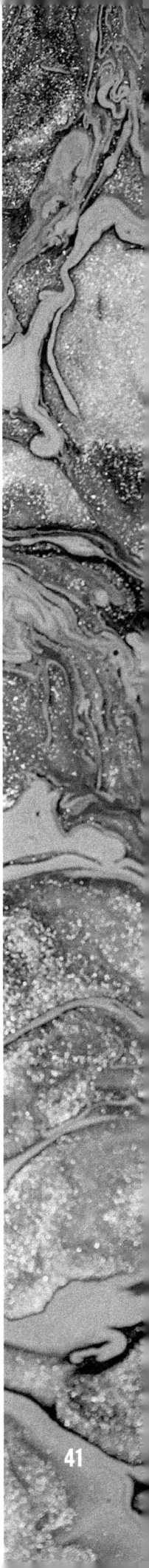

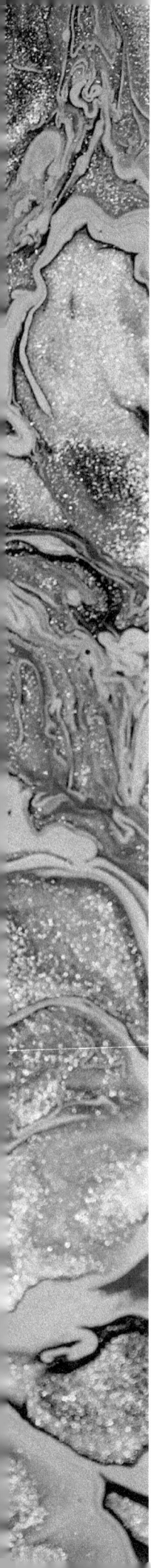

Chapter 5

Are You Ready to Model a Growth Mindset?

"Live as if you were to die tomorrow;
learn as if you were to live forever."

Mahatma Gandhi

Tony Robbins notes that human beings have four basic needs: certainty, uncertainty or variety, significance, and connection. The other two human needs are more spiritual—growth and contribution. For an organization to have an extraordinary emergent culture, a growth mindset needs to be in the living, being, and behaving of the organization. To truly embody a growth mindset, it must be ingrained in the culture and behavior. This section is meant to inspire you toward that growth mindset.

The focus here is on the importance of choosing to live with a growth mindset and how to incorporate it into your organization's culture. When new ideas come along, you can't just say, "Oh, we can't do that, and here's why." If you're striving for organizational excellence, a growth mindset is the only way to get there. When a company adopts a growth mindset, managers see more leadership, creativity, collaboration and innovation from their employees.

So, what exactly is a growth mindset? It's the belief that our abilities and intelligence can be developed and improved over time through dedication and hard work. It means embracing challenges and learning from failures rather than avoiding them out of the fear of looking incompetent.

Growth Mindset   **Fixed Mindset**

GROWTH, WE CAN!
I CAN! How can I?
What is possible? I will find a way!
I MAY NEED TO SHIFT.
I need to get curious. I am in control
I AM NOT MY   of my thoughts.
THOUGHTS. I am not my past.
I may have some beliefs that are
limiting myself and my potential.
I AM A CREATOR.
I try new things for fun.
I enjoy stretch
projects.

I REACT.
You made me.
After all I have been through.
It is your fault.   WHY ME?
If they would just......
THIS AGAIN? It will never work.
If it were not for these people.......
MY PAST DETERMINES MY FUTURE.
CHANGE IS SO HARD.
I am a reactor.
I KNOW THAT
ALREADY.

This is the opposite of a fixed mindset. Those with a fixed mindset believe that a person's abilities, intelligence, and talents are innate, fixed, and unchangeable. The behaviors of those with a fixed mindset especially show up when it comes to challenges and failure. People with fixed mindsets tend to put in minimal effort, and they give up easily when faced with an obstacle.

Those with a growth mindset, on the other hand, see challenges as an opportunity to problem solve, and they see failure as an opportunity to learn. They're always striving to improve. They're open to new ideas and new ways of doing things. You can't fake a growth-mindset culture. As the leader, you must embody it. You need to commit to learning, leaning in with a beginner's mind, collaborating, and being appreciative of the ideas and perspectives of others. When you do this, you are naturally inspired by others' growth.

As a leader, it's important to reflect on your own behavior and how it aligns with a growth mindset. You'll examine how you respond to new ideas. Do you use failure as a learning opportunity? Do you actively seek out new ideas and perspectives, even if they challenge the status quo? Do you include people in ideation sessions to encourage their input? Do you celebrate the successes of others within your organization? These are all critical elements of a growth mindset.

If you're starting from a more fixed mindset, you'll likely need to retrain your brain for growth and change. To lay the groundwork for increased neuroplasticity, you'll focus on eight key areas:

- Quality sleep
- Improved diet
- More exercise
- Train your brain to focus on doing only one thing at a time
- Calm your brain
- Try out reading, experiencing and exploring new places and things
- Practice gratitude
- Engage in deep experiential observation

To help you with this, you'll complete an exercise in the form of a wheel chart to track these key areas. We invite you to track your progress on this wheel for one week to see how you're doing in each area, as these elements are essential to your overall well-being and growth mindset. To nurture a growth-mindset culture, it is important that you model what it is to be a person with self-awareness of your emotions and behaviors To achieve breakthrough success for yourself and your company, understanding that change is often uncomfortable for people allows you to engage them in the practice of learning to be comfortable being uncomfortable.

8 KEYS TO NEUROPLASTICITY

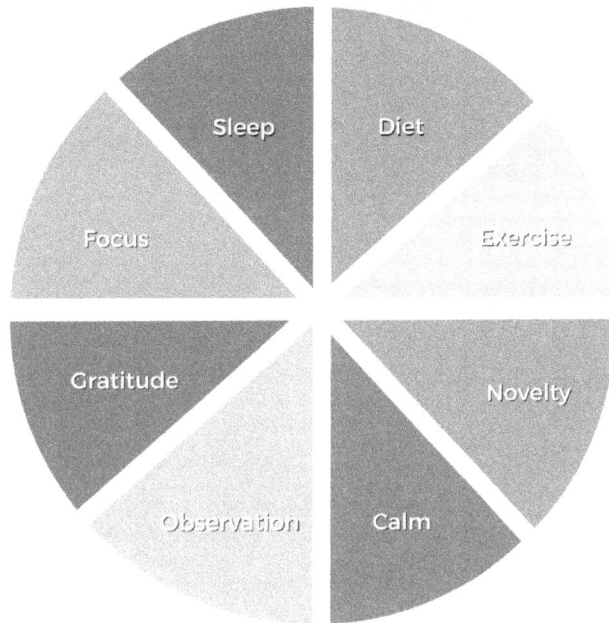

In addition to these exercises, we offer a bonus exercise, focused on listening, that you can complete on your own time. We want to make sure that we don't overload you with too much information, and we also want to give you the tools you need to develop a growth mindset and become the best version of yourself.

You'll end this section with an exercise on gratitude. Take a few moments for a meditation on gratitude to reflect on what you're grateful for and what's working in your life. This will help you end on a positive note and set the stage for the next section. So let's dive in and start building or deepening a growth-mindset and modeling it for others. Remember, a growth mindset is not just something you say but something you live and breathe. Let's make it happen!

Neurotransmitters that form and reorganize synaptic connections:

• Serotonin
• Oxytocin
• Dopamine
• Endorphins

Questions to Consider:

Do you have a growth mindset? How do you know?

Do you like to try new things?

What was the last new thing you learned?

How long did it take you to learn it?

What emotions do you experience when things don't go as planned?

Are you collaborative?

How do you know?

Where do you find that you collaborate best?

What kind of people do you collaborate best with?

Are you appreciative of others' ideas?

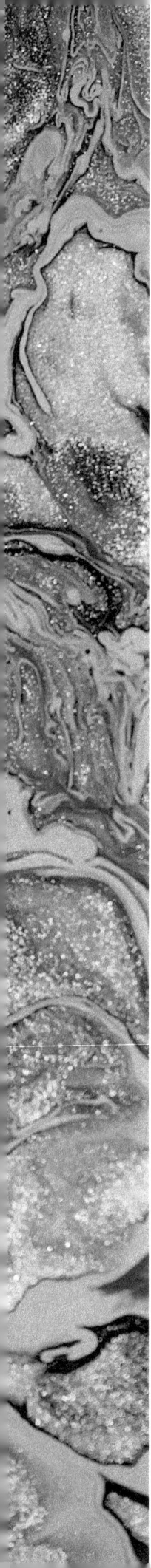

Chapter 6
Paving the Way for Breakthrough Performance

"A breakthrough occurs when you recognize
you are more energy than matter."

Caroline Myss

Foundationally, no major breakthroughs have come from self-limiting beliefs; they begin with a vision. To bring those breakthroughs to your organization, you'll need an inspiring way to share your vision. Welcome to chapter 6 of the *Ignite Culture* guidebook and master class. You've done a lot of work to get this far, and now you'll be bringing it all together to focus on the importance of how you communicate your vision, really listen, and connect to achieve breakthrough performance.

Breakthroughs are significant leaps forward in what is possible. To get there, you first have to be able to control the self-limiting behaviors in your own life and start living your vision before you are able to bring that to your team. You have to get honest about everything that's in the way and everything that holds you back. That starts with yourself, not others.

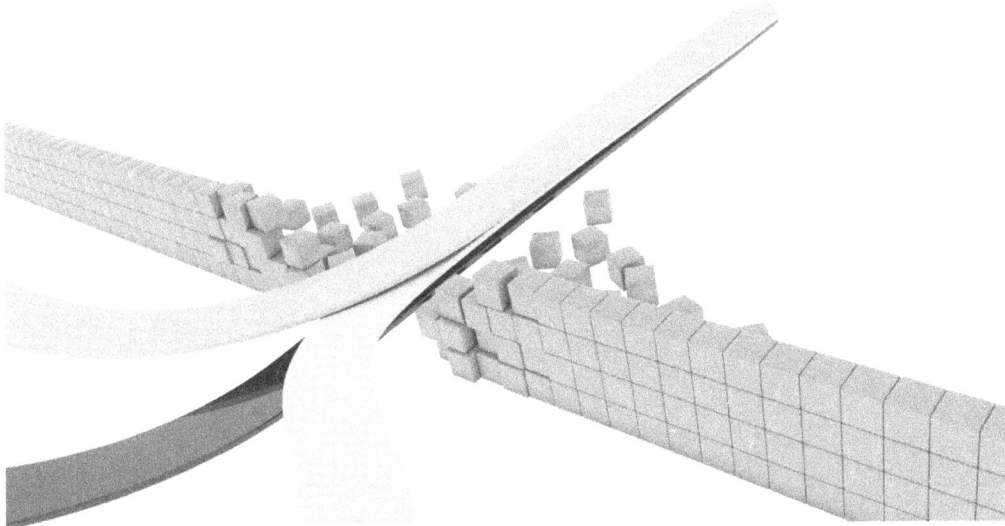

It is time for you to make a declaration. It is time to declare your vision, own it, put your stake in the ground, and align your life to it. Soon, we'll invite you to do an exercise to declare your vision, share it with another person, and then fully listen to the feedback from all areas. Once your vision is declared, it is time to hold yourself accountable and maintain your integrity to doing what is needed to operate in alignment with that vision.

After you complete the Vision exercise, we will work with you on honing the art of enrolling others in that vision. By practicing how you declare your vision and elicit input you gain mastery at elevating your teams understanding of your big WHY. In the process, you also gain their buy-in.

It is important to address your internal and external communication. You will need to be responsible for your self-talk and all the automatic negative thoughts that are occurring for you every day, while also addressing your external communication to become more intentional and effective at inspiring change.

Communications Intelligence

Remember from *The Three Laws of Performance* that there are simple principles that drive breakthrough performance. The first principle is to understand that how people perform correlates to how situations occur to them. Basically, what people believe about a given situation or how it occurs for them dictates how they will respond. If they think something is impossible, it likely will not be possible for them. Past experiences shape these beliefs and in turn, these beliefs shape how people behave and how they perform. To change behavior or performance, a person must first change their belief or how the situation occurs to them. As a leader, the only way you can do that is to help people to recognize that their future can be different. To do that will require a lot of deep listening on your part.

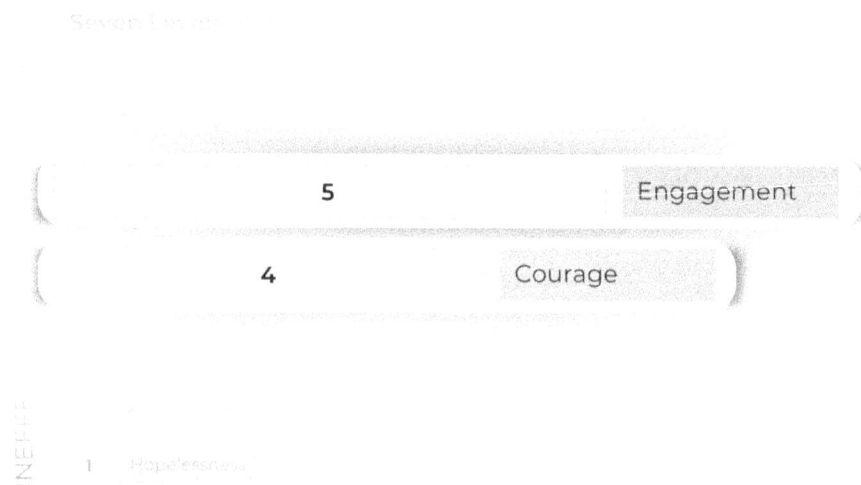

5	Engagement	
4	Courage	

The second principle is to acknowledge that how situations occur arises in language. The type of language used significantly impacts our thoughts and behaviors because language is how we share our beliefs and life experiences. To bring others into your vision of the future, you must align your communication with your vision and help others understand where they fit in. Again, this will take a lot of deep listening and undoubtedly some training and support.

The final principle here is that future-based language transforms how situations occur to people. To impact the future of your company, you must shift people's perceptions of what can be possible in the future. As a leader, it's important to support people in creating a vision of their own that aligns their personal values and purpose. When employees intrinsic motivation is turned on inside of work, magic happens. Next, encourage those people to be curious about how their contribution to your organizational mission brings them closer to personal fulfillment.

The thread that runs throughout each of these principles is listening. Listening is a crucial aspect of effective communication that is often overlooked. Soon, you'll do an exercise that will support you in practicing listening skills. You'll have subjects to talk about with other people, and you'll practice through the five levels of listening we discussed earlier:

- not listening or ignoring
- pretending to listen
- only hearing what you want or selective hearing
- engaged or attentive
- listening from your heart or empathetic listening

As stated in the *Ignite Culture Book*, "The more personal development you have done to strengthen your higher self and align your thoughts and behaviors with your personal values and vision, the more likely you are to experience personal and professional breakthroughs." You've examined and shaken off what has been holding you back. Now it's time to help others do the same. Moving from personal alignment to group alignment means mastering communication. Communication is everything when it comes to inspiring breakthrough performance.

By supporting the individuals on your teams to develop themselves, you strengthen the humans and the human systems in your company. In sharing your vision while listening to theirs, you create a shared vision together. You'll listen more deeply and communicate more constructively. A bond of trust and an atmosphere of respect and collaboration is formed. The way others listen and communicate evolves as well. So, let's get started with the listening exercise and declare your vision for your organization.

Your Vision

What is your vision?

What are you doing each day to work toward that vision?

What takes you off track of living in alignment with that vision?

Communicating Your Vision

How do you communicate your vision?

What do you say?

What do you leave out?

Why?

Practice Session: Practice the Four Levels of Listening

Think of a situation at work that is not working as well as you'd like it to.

Write it down.

Find a partner and practice the four levels of listening as you discuss the problem.

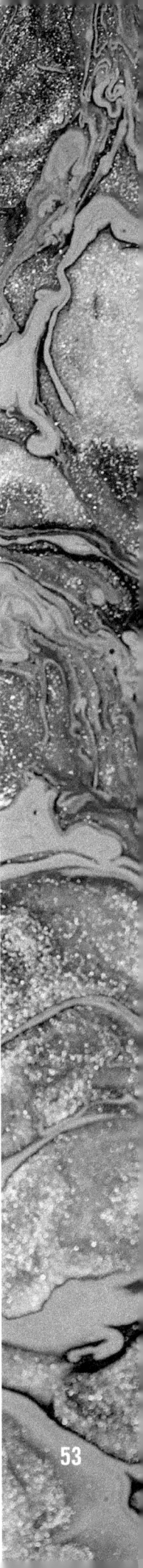

1. Listening from habits (not really listening)

https://www.trainerslibrary.org/are-you-really-listening/

2. Listening from outside (allow yourself to have an open mind).

3. Listening from within (allow yourself to connect and listen with your heart).

4. Listening from infinite intelligence (allow yourself to listen from an open will and from what is possible).

High Support

```
┌─────────────────┐              ┌─────────────────┐
│                 │              │                 │
│   Status Quo    │              │   Performance   │
│                 │              │    Catalyst     │
│ "How we've always│             │ Always improving│
│  done it" culture│             │ culture –Strategy is│
│                 │              │   inevitable    │
└─────────────────┘              └─────────────────┘
```

Low Challenge ─────────────────────────────── High Challenge

```
┌─────────────────┐              ┌─────────────────┐
│                 │              │                 │
│   Depressive    │              │  Fear & Self-   │
│   Dead Zone     │              │   Protection    │
│                 │              │                 │
│  Entropy rules  │              │  Manipulation,  │
│     culture     │              │ avoidance & self-│
│                 │              │ interested culture│
└─────────────────┘              └─────────────────┘
```

Low Support

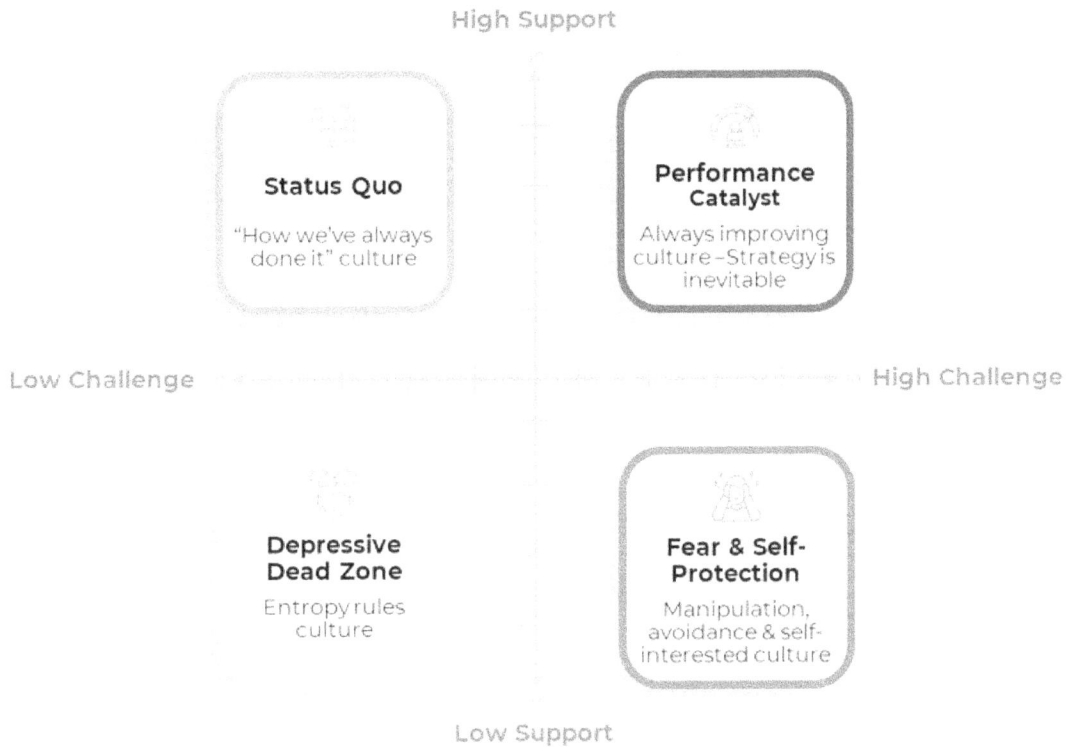

Is your Organization Operating in the Performance Catalyst Zone?

Rate where you think your team and organization is on the graph and ask your peers to rate where they think the team and organization are as well. Then compare and contrast. Have an open conversation about why they rated what they rated, and what they think would support the team to move to a higher level.

Your Team

How will you share the personal work you have done with the team that you spend the most time with?

Three Laws of Performance - Zaffron and Logan and Building Trust - Flores and Solomon

1. People respond based on their perceptions. Past experiences shape beliefs, moods, assumptions, and how we perceive the future. This is the default future. **As a leader you need to help people rewrite their default future.**

What questions can you ask to support you in understanding what moods and attitudes your team has about the future?

2. How situations occur arises in language. Words matter. Tonality matters. We need to align our communication style, tonality, and language with our vision. **Craft your message and practice it**. We recommend practicing in the mirror or in front of a safe audience that will give you honest feedback.

What message do you want to deliver?

What future do you want to create?

How can you use this opportunity to write this message in a compelling, clear, and concise way?

3. Future-based language transforms how situations occur to people. **Envision the future and inspire people to lean in, contribute, and be part of it.**

How can you deliver your message in a way that makes people want to participate, contribute, and be part of the new future and the solution?

Closing for Leaders

You've arrived at the conclusion of our section for leaders. We've covered a lot of ground, and we believe you found this guidebook and master class informative and transformative. Our goal in this first section was to help you understand the importance of culture in your team and organization and to provide you with the tools and knowledge you need to spark excitement for cultivating an intentional, healthy, high-performance organization from the inside out. Bravo for beginning with yourself. You are the catalyst for positive internal change and others will certainly model your behavior and attitude.

As a leader, you set the tone for your team and play a critical role in shaping the behaviors and attitudes that define your culture. Remember that culture is not something that happens by chance; it is something that you, as the leader, must intentionally create and nurture. Your role is to set the tone for an emergent culture and to ensure that everyone in your organization is aligned with the compelling cause and inspiring values you have invented.

A healthy culture doesn't just benefit you, or even your team, it also drives success for your organization as a whole. So, take the first step by starting conversations with your team and committing to creating an ideal culture. Keep an open mind, be receptive to feedback, and be willing to adjust when necessary.

Remember, culture is a journey, not a destination. It requires ongoing attention and investment, and the rewards are significant. By cultivating an environment that aligns with your values and supports your goals, you unlock and unleash the full potential of your team and achieve extraordinary results.

We're here to support you every step of the way.

I encourage you to take the lessons you have learned in this section and apply them to your own leadership style. Lead by example and be the change you want to see in your organization. Thank you for joining us in this journey, and I wish you all the best on your path to ignite an emergent culture of high performance.

Section 2

The Leadership Team—Is It Impaired or Inspired?

Welcome and Introduction

Welcome leadership team. I'm glad you are here for the *Ignite Culture* guidebook and master class. This section is specifically focused on you. I am certain you are feeling inspired to take action towards a positive cultural shift. Culture is the hot topic, however it can also seem elusive and nebulous. As a team, you need answers. One of the most important things you will do is to understand what is causing destructive friction in the human system. Whether it's personalities on overdrive, systemic mistrust, poor conversations for action resulting in low accountability, clunky handoffs, or breakdowns in communication. All of the aforementioned issues cause distress to employees and clog workflows. Proactively taking the time and effort to get curious about constraints in the system is key to eradicating unwanted employee turnover, shrinking profit margins, customer churn, and market-share erosion.

Throughout this next section, you'll have the opportunity to better understand alignment and trust within the leadership team. Whereas the previous sections were to support you in getting aligned and clear about your own WHY and the roadblocks that often get in the way of breakthrough performance, the next section is about getting the leadership team on the same page. This gives you all the environment of trust that is the foundation of organizational performance.

The organization is relying on you. One person can't do all the work of transformation on their own; it takes a team of people who are united in service of cultivating an environment where emergence and innovation is a way of being. Are you ready to dive into igniting that culture for your team and everyone you impact? Let's get going!

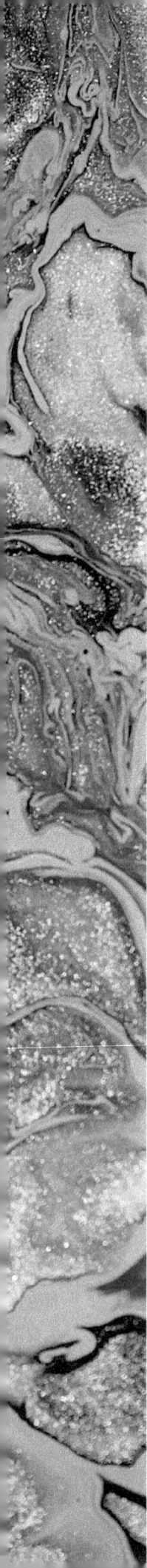

Chapter 7
What Got You Here Isn't Enough to Break Through

It is time to focus on you and how to expand the emergent mindset throughout your team and beyond. As a team, it is important that you are ready for all the change that your organization needs to navigate in the next decade. The only way to cultivate an environment that is fertile ground for change is to continue to nurture and ready the human system; beginning with your team, to thrive through change.

The first step in this transformation process is to understand what is required for a healthy, intentional and high performance human system to thrive. There are 4 key components required for an emergent culture to form and sustain high levels of engagement and productivity.

- High Levels of Achievement in service of delivering on your Noble Cause & emerging genius in the system.
- An environment and architecture that supports the Self Actualization of the people in the system.
- An environment that supports humanistic/encouraging behaviors such as genuine care and respect for one another.
- An environment and architecture that supports effective teamwork, affiliation & collaboration.

In this chapter, you'll be taking a closer look at your leadership team to evaluate how real these components are in the day-to-day interactions among your team. You'll complete a leadership inventory and delve into how aligned your team is on the goals. You will assess to what degree the leadership team members experience self-actualization in their roles. Additionally, you'll evaluate how well your team treats each other, trusts each other and supports each other. Lastly you'll look at how effectively your team affiliates and collaborates with one another and brings new ideas to fruition as a team. All of this inquiry will illuminate what is working on your leadership team as well as what is not working or not working as well as it could. It is crucial that you tell the truth here and that you do not let artificial harmony cloud your judgement. As a famous visionary, poet, and liberator once said, "the truth shall set you free."

Finally, you will be assessing and evaluating how your team makes decisions, how effective those decisions are, and what could make the team even stronger at decision making. We'll be offering an assessment for each member of the team to take, which

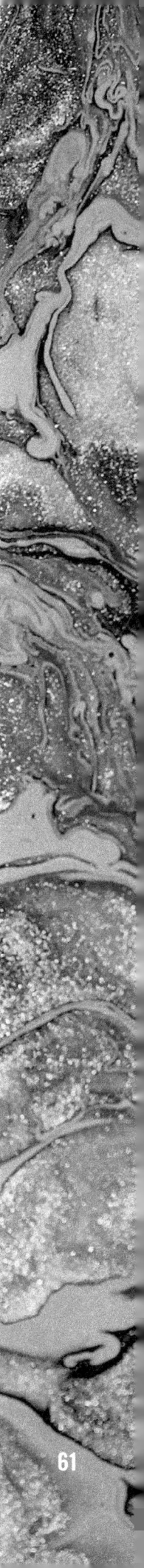

will help uncover any unworkability or constraint that may be present in the team. You are invited to explore some of the most common dysfunctions we see, including:

- Silo mentality – Withholding information and impeding collaboration.
- Fiefdom syndrome – Overly focusing on the success of a particular area or group to the detriment of others.
- Win-lose mindset – A noncollaborative way of believing that there are only right and wrong ways to do things.
- Passive-aggressive behavior – Refusing to address underlying negative feelings.
- Perfectionism – Causing the micromanagement of everything.
- Cordial hypocrisy – Pretending there is trust or loyalty where there isn't.
- Systemic distrust – The majority of the people simply don't trust leadership.

The goal here is to assess the team's current behavioral patterns and competencies and to identify any areas for improvement. This type of inquiry serves to uncover how the team's behavior may unintentionally be thwarting effectiveness. This workbook provides you with questions that aid you in your assessment.

You may want to consider inviting your leadership team to take the Saboteur Assessment from Positive Intelligence. https://www.positiveintelligence.com/saboteurs/

This wonderful free tool gives leaders a look see how their strengths, when overused, get in their way and cause problems for themselves and those they work with and lead.

Once the current behaviors and constraints are identified, it's time for a deep alignment. Any distrust within the leadership team needs to be addressed and repaired. Alliances need to be created. Extreme ownership for cultivating trust and restoring it when it is broken is required from each and every member on the team.

If you need support, my team does this work in powerful, experiential workshops. Whether you take it upon yourselves or with support, as a team you need to find a way to make a complete demarcation from the old, dysfunctional ways of behaving to the new, inspired, emergent culture that is being ushered in. You need to fully understand what is needed to fulfill the organization's highest purpose and bring the entire human system toward growth.

After completing this section, you will have a clear understanding of the leadership team's strengths and weaknesses and will be able to take steps towards cultivating an environment of trust and engagement. This type of environment spurs positive energy and is fertile ground for people to grow, expand their capacity for new challenges, and thrive. You and your team will complete this work with eyes and hearts wide open and you will be ready to influence others in the organization to do the same. We're glad you're joining us. Let's get started!

Honest Evaluation of Your Leadership Team

Where do the people on your leadership team need development? On a scale of one to ten, rate each person in each category. Use the chart below to fill in the names and the scores.

1. **Envisioning an Outcome:** Leading begins with realizing and clearly envisioning the overall mission to accomplish. A mission is what is going to happen, not how. Realizing your mission leads to the understanding of where change is required and why it is needed now.

2. **Understanding Your Supporters:** Understanding how your vision satisfies people's perceived needs is crucial to engage them. You must know what changes others are receptive to and ready for. Listening carefully and objectively will ensure that your mission is one that others will embrace.

3. **Communicating Your Vision:** In order to engage people to follow your vision, you must clearly communicate it to them. The most powerful movements for change are created by people who have an emotional commitment to the mission and are passionate about it. Therefore, you must be able to communicate with people not just through logical arguments, but in a way that touches them emotionally.

4. **Serving Others:** People will not chase a difficult dream for very long unless they think it supports their own personal goals. You must ensure that people connect both your vision and your actions with their own goals.

5. **Inspiring Others:** Embarking on difficult and uncertain journeys requires a special kind of energy in order to continue for the long term. People become inspired when they start believing they have more ability than they thought they did. Therefore, leading includes challenging people to do more than they have before and empowering them to make efforts that will yield a positive result.

6. **Guiding Others:** In taking action and moving toward completion of your mission and vision, there will inevitably be surprises and unexpected results. A person skilled in leading will continually assess the plan for achieving the stated goals and make corrections along the way. Leading requires a focus on the milestones along the way, not just on the long-term mission. Followers require some indication that they are on the right track, and this builds confidence in the leader.

7. **Developing Yourself:** In order to understand, motivate, and lead others, you must first understand yourself. So, before a person can lead others, they must lead the way. Leaders must practice what they preach and be able to see and develop themselves before they can do so for others.

Name	Score						
	Envisioning an Outcome	Understanding Your Supporters	Communicating Your Vision	Serving Others	Inspiring Others	Guiding Others	Developing Yourself

Where is there conflict on the leadership team?

Is it healthy or unhealthy?

How do you know?

What is your vision for change?

What are your milestones?

Who are you enlisting to support you in leading the change?

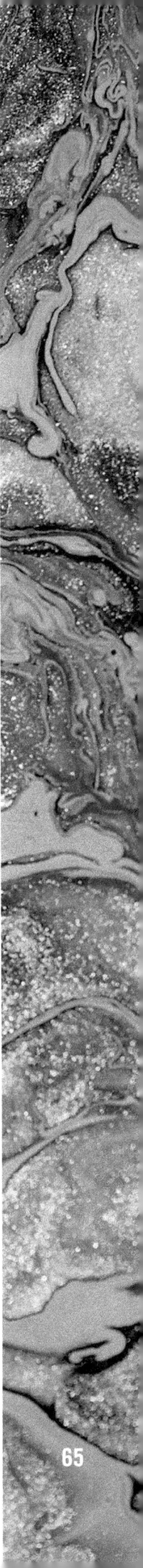

What structures do you need in place to move things forward and keep the lines of communication open?

What behavioral agreements need to be in place to realize positive, lasting change?

What are the consequences for keeping agreements and the consequences for breaking agreements?

How will you respond to broken agreements?

How will you celebrate success?

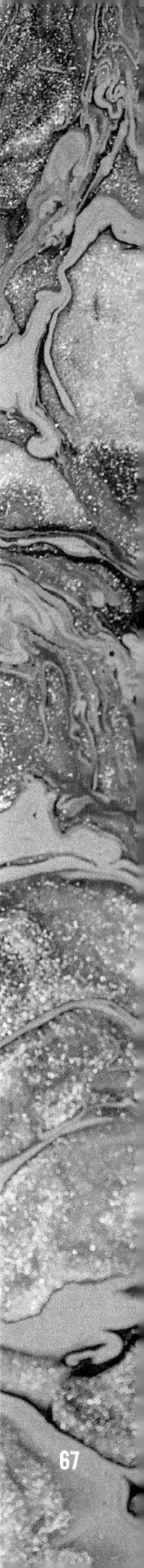

Business Life Cycle

10 STAGES OF A BUSINESS LIFECYCLE

"At the foundation of effective management for any organization is the fundamental truth that all organizations like all organisms, have a lifecycle and undergo very predictable and repetitive behavior as they grow and develop." – I Adizes

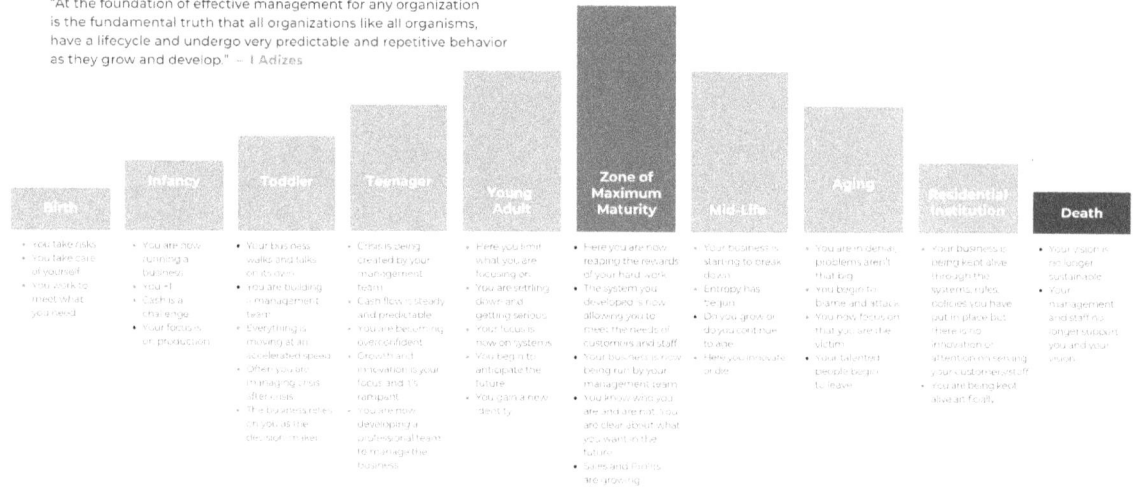

Birth
- You take risks
- You take care of yourself
- You work to meet what you need

Infancy
- You are now running a business
- You +1
- Cash is a challenge
- Your focus is on production

Toddler
- Your business walks and talks on its own
- You are building a management team
- Everything is moving at an accelerated speed
- After you quit thinking and discussing
- The business relies on you as the decision maker

Teenager
- Crisis is being created by your management team
- Cash flow is steady and predictable
- You are becoming overconfident
- Growth and innovation is your focus and it's rampant
- You are now developing a professional team to manage the business

Young Adult
- Here you limit what you are focusing on
- You are settling down and getting serious
- Your focus is now on systems
- You keep in to anticipate the future
- You gain a new identity

Zone of Maximum Maturity
- Here you are now reaping the rewards of your hard work
- The system you developed is now allowing you to meet the needs of customers and staff
- Your business is now being run by your management team
- You know who you are and are not. You are clear about what you want in the future
- Sales and Profits are growing

Mid-Life
- Your business is starting to break down
- Entropy has begun
- Do you grow or do you continue to age
- Here you innovate or die

Aging
- You are in denial, problems aren't that big
- You begin to blame and attack
- You now focus on that you are the victim
- Your talented people begin to leave

Residential Institution
- Your business is being kept alive through the systems, rules, policies you have put in place but there is no innovation or attention to serving your customers or staff
- You are being kept alive artificially

Death
- Your vision is no longer sustainable
- Your management and staff no longer support you and your vision

---

What life cycle is your organization in?

Why do you believe it is this way?

68

What stage would the rest of the leadership team say your organizational department is at?

Now that you see what you see, what conversations do you need to have?

What do you need to improve, repair, or build to move to the next stage?

What Team Dysfunction is harming your Organization's Culture?

1. Silo Mentality
2. Fiefdom Syndrome
3. Win-Lose Mindset
4. Passive-Aggressive Behavior
5. Perfectionism (Controlling / Micromanaging)
6. Cordial Hypocrisy
7. Systemic Distrust

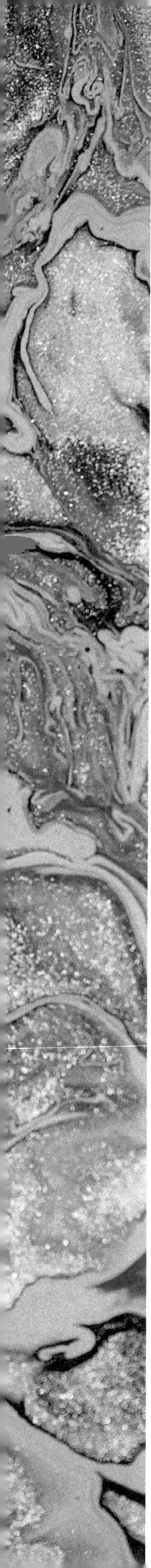

Chapter 8
Alignment Is the Key to Sustainability

*"Every time you are tempted to react in the same old way,
ask if you want to be a prisoner of the past or a pioneer of the future."*

Deepak Chopra

Now that the leadership team has delved deeply into the personal and group dynamics to address any underlying issues that impede forward progress, it is time to start setting the framework for transformation beyond your team. It is time to align. In this chapter, you'll see the importance of alignment in achieving and sustaining high levels of success for the long term.

The leadership team will need to have ongoing personal and professional support, as well as training to be able to support positive, lasting change. It is the only way they will be able to ensure that an emergent team continues to evolve. Along with tending to the environment, it is imperative that your team designs the kind of architecture that allows each member to fully contribute, learn, grow, explore, fail, and thrive. A part of that architecture must include a structure for making and keeping agreements.

Let's start by talking about trust, which is one of the key components of alignment. There are three types of trust: simple trust, blind trust, and authentic trust. Simple trust is when you trust someone because they have always been trustworthy, without any further discernment. Blind trust is when you place trust in someone without really knowing them. Authentic trust is when you have a deep understanding of someone and their character and you trust them based on that. Authentic trust is critical for building strong teams, and it requires personal responsibility for all members of the team. Creating the environment for authentic trust to flourish is no easy task. It is an ongoing process of building trust, acknowledging where trust is broken, and restoring trust. When this is a fundamental element to the way your team works with each other, there will be no stopping you.

This important foundational work of building trust is critical for getting your leadership team into deep alignment. Doing the personal work as a leader and going through a process of deep alignment as a team can help you eliminate any volatility, uncertainty, chaos, and ambiguity (VUCA) among yourselves. Only after that foundational work is done can you and your team move into achieving breakthrough performance.

Once the leader and leadership team are deeply aligned, you're ready to intentionally and honestly begin co-creating your strategic plan and design a compelling future for

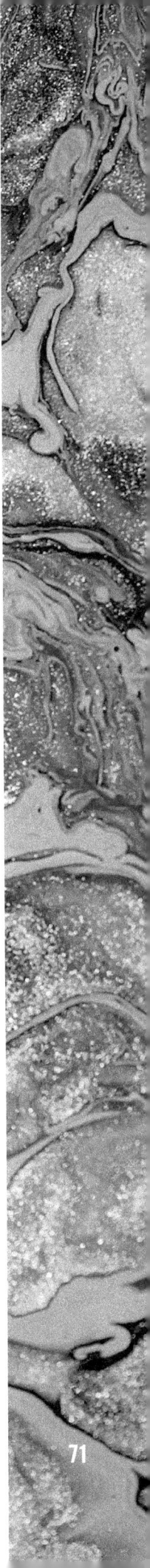

your organization. In this chapter, we'll look at the road map to continue down your path of alignment. For deeper assistance with this, you can go through an immersive strategy session with my team. However it is done, the road map needs to allow your team to:

- Ideate and align on the organizations' Noble Cause, as well as its inspiring, compelling Mission, Vision, and Values.
- Agree on how decisions will be made through well-defined strategic anchors.
- Align the leadership team around a thematic goal.
- Gain new perspectives on the power of accountability and integrity as a new way of being that ignites a thriving, healthy, high-performance culture.

Starting with a Noble Cause and an inspiring mission allows the team to rally around a new compelling future. Without a Noble Cause, your human system lacks the higher intent to align on and focus their efforts towards. Without a powerful cause people have a hard time understanding the big picture of how the work they do serves the whole. A noble cause is the higher purpose of a team, and it's what drives them forward. Your Noble Cause is the reason your team exists and what it aims to achieve.

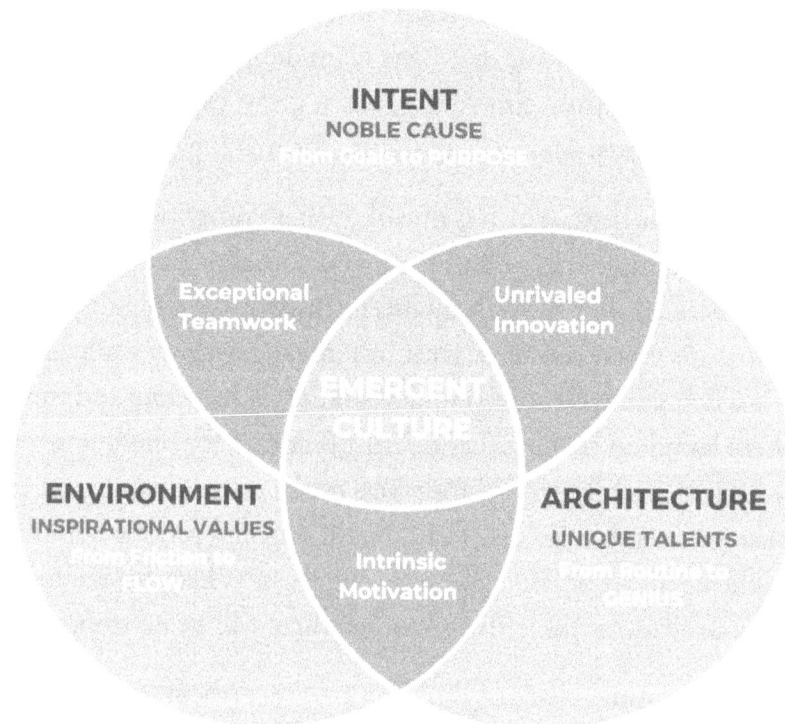

You can see how your organization's shared values shape the behavior in the environment, leading to exceptional teamwork in service of your Noble Cause. You can also see that architecture designed specifically to optimize how unique talents are expressed is where intrinsic motivation and unrivaled motivation blossom.

It's also important to agree on how you will achieve your noble cause, which is where strategic anchors come into play. These are the overarching strategies that will guide your organization toward its noble cause. Strategic anchors distill the core values of your organization right down to their very essence. Having these anchors in place speeds up the time for decision-making because the impact of an opportunity or threat can be seen so clearly.

A Thematic goal supports your leadership team in focusing on one singular initiative or body of work for a period of time. There are no specific numbers attached to a thematic goal. It is a shared vision for the team to direct action and attention toward ONE FOCUS for a set period of time. It brings focus and rallies the team around a purpose, encouraging the team to work together.

This whole process needs to be very intentional. You need to remain accountable to ensure alignment is sustained. Accountability is crucial for ensuring that the team stays aligned and focused on achieving its goals. By considering and taking these steps along your road map, you can achieve alignment within your organization and have sustainable success as you work toward your Noble Cause. Intentional alignment is the key to high performance. Let's get started!

Noble Cause

What is your organizational noble cause?

How is the world better because of what your company does?

Mission

What is your company's mission?

What does your company actually do?

Who do you serve?

What are your core competencies and how do they show up in how you serve?

How is your company unique?

What do you guarantee?

Values

What are your core values? How are they operationalized? Are they aspirational or inspirational? How do you know?

What behaviors exemplify your core values?

How do you demonstrate them?

What behaviors impede your people from being true to your company's values?

Do you know the values by heart?

Does everyone else know the values by heart?

How often do you discuss the core values with team members?

.

What are the structures you utilize to weave the core values through communications, meetings, and day-to-day operations?

Thematic Goals

What is the overarching SPRINT your organization will take on this quarter, half year, or year?

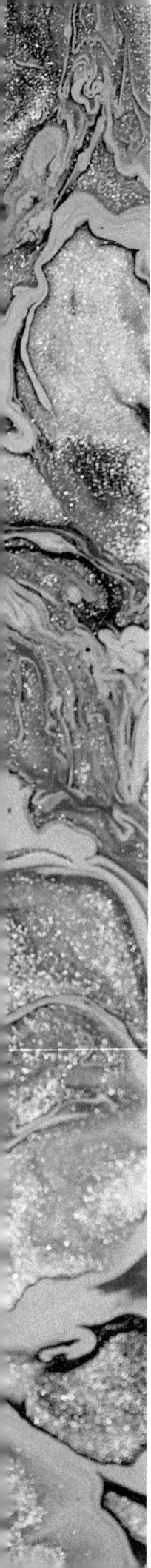

Chapter 9

Trust is the Foundation of a High-Performance Team

Who do you trust right now? Do you trust the government? The media? Your board? Your colleagues? Edelman's Trust Barometer measures the level of trust in major institutions, businesses, and governments around the world. Right now, the credibility of corporate leaders is at an all-time low. Trust deeply affects your organization, and it could be a complete game changer if you get it right.

Remember the three types of trust discussed in the previous section: simple trust, blind trust, and authentic trust. Let's take a closer look at each.

Simple trust is just an unintentional habit based on assumptions and first instincts without much thought given, if any. You trust someone because they've always been trustworthy, without any further discernment. For example, you trust that mail will be delivered on weekdays, and you trust your coworkers to show up to work even though they may or may not.

Most organizations have blind trust. This is when someone immediately does business with another person without checking who they really are. This often leads to unfulfilled expectations. For example, let's say you're working on a project with a colleague you've never worked with before. You immediately like them and assume they have the same work style as you. You don't really have a conversation about how you'll work together, what your expectations are, or what your individual responsibilities will be. As the project progresses, you notice that your colleague isn't meeting deadlines and their work is subpar. You get frustrated and upset, but you don't talk to them about it. Instead, you put up blockers like withholding information or avoiding them altogether. Your colleague senses that something's off, but they're not sure what it is. They feel like you don't trust them, and they become defensive. The project suffers, and you both become resentful.

With authentic trust, clear and consistent communication is required, along with accountability for your word and agreements. Conversations should be had when things are not done as agreed, without shaming or blaming. In the example above, if you had started with authentic trust, you would have had an open and honest conversation about your expectations and how you work best. You would have been clear about your responsibilities and deadlines and made sure that you were on the same page. If something went wrong, you would have had a conversation and worked together to find a solution. You would have stayed focused on the goal of the project and made sure that you were both accountable for your individual contributions. In the end, the project would have been more successful, and you would have built a stronger relationship with your colleague based on mutual trust and respect.

Building authentic trust in an organization requires personal responsibility by all team members. Once that trust is deeply established, everything changes for the better. To get to authentic trust, any areas of mistrust must first be cleaned up. Acknowledge, recommit, and repromise in any areas that are currently falling short. Repromising what will get done is more important than focusing on why it wasn't done in the first place. With authentic trust in place, everyone is clear who is doing what and when. There is also clarity about the consequences and rewards for completing work as promised.

Cordial hypocrisy is another aspect of trust that should be addressed here. This occurs when everyone pretends everything is great, but there is really collusion and "meetings" after your meetings. Like in the previous example of blind trust, the real issues aren't being addressed and troubles arise because of this.

So, it's time for some personal inquiry into your accountability, because trust comes from doing what you say you are going to do. Look at your goals from last year, last quarter, or last month. Did you accomplish them? How about the goals of your team? Did they complete theirs? Ask yourself how you hold yourself accountable. How do you deal with unattained goals? Do you have conversations with people to work through what didn't get done? Is there any clean up needed? Are there any agreements that need realigning and re-promising?

The key takeaway is that trust is foundational and necessary for success. Without trust, change will not happen. Trust comes from accountability. You need to have conversations to repromise on any unfulfilled goals and agreements. Authentic trust doesn't just magically happen; it's the result of continuous attention and nurturing. Everyone needs to commit to personal responsibility, and the leadership team needs to commit as an organization, otherwise authentic trust will never be developed. It is only with authentic trust that an organization can achieve breakthrough performance.

Once this base of authentic trust is established, you'll be able to focus on a structure for clearing any roadblocks. Let's do this!

What is the impact of VUCA on your team?

Systemic Distrust

What is happening in the organization that leaves people wondering?

Building Trust

What is your organization doing to ensure your employees are kept informed, up-to-date, and aware as changes occur?

Where do you thrive in this?

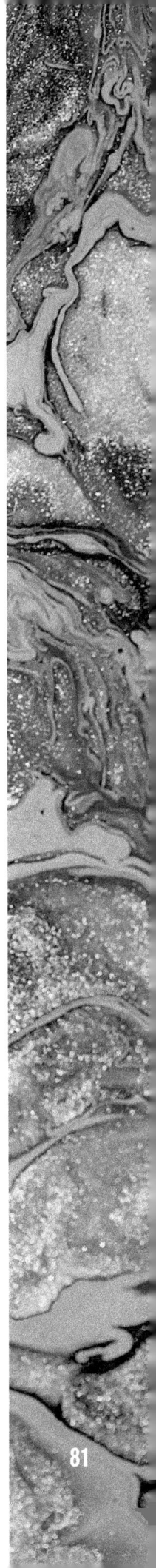

Where do you need to improve in this?

Cordial Hypocrisy

Where in the organization is cordial hypocrisy the standard way of being?

Where is smiling and saying yes expected?

Where should you be questioning and introducing open, honest, authentic dialogue?

Chapter 10
A Structure for Dismantling Roadblocks

Things won't always go according to plan, and it's important to be able to identify and declare a breakdown when it occurs so you can move beyond it. This means acknowledging that something isn't working and digging in to figure out why or what is getting in the way of success. This chapter supports you in dismantling the roadblocks in your team/organization in order to move through the inevitable breakdowns with more speed and ease.

Typically, an organization has one person in charge of finance, another in charge of IT, and yet another in charge of operations. But, when there's an emergency or when the company is taking a step backward, it doesn't matter who's in charge of what. Everyone needs to rally together to get things fixed. When there is a breakdown, if it puts the organization in a state of emergency or danger, one leader needs to step in to navigate the problem until the situation is resolved and things are back on track. If there are too many people chiming in, volatility, uncertainty, confusion and ambiguity will likely be the result and that will not solve the crisis. One leader is highly recommended until the problem is resolved.

If it's the first breakdown, that's one thing, but if it's consistently not being handled, the leader (head honcho) needs to step in. A customer my organization worked with had a systemic breakdown with one of their divisions. The person in charge continued to tell the other executive team members that he was on track to solve this problem. While the Exec in charge of this problem was out of the country everything blew up and a very large and significant customer threatened to defect over the unresolved issue. By the time the issue hit the CEO's desk it was far too late to get to the root cause of the problem. The unresolved issue wound up costing the organization over a million dollars to solve, as well as the good will in the customer relationship, the trust of other departments and the reputation of the Executive, who was later terminated. At the end of the day the CEO himself had to step in and manage the resolution. Depending on the gravity of the situation, the leader may have to intervene to ensure the breakdown is handled. It is important to be mindful of what it could be costing your company and then either step in and take charge or give the problem to the right people to solve.

If your organization's human system is learning by failing forward, your organization will be better equipped to win. Using liberating structures, which are techniques that disrupt how people work together and empower the people closest to the problem to solve it, allows you to shift the way you relate to problems and grants the power of innovation. Building architecture that supports the optimization of the collective genius of the human system creates an environment ripe for problem solving and innovation.

There are more than 30 liberating structures that can be leveraged to empower and tap into new ideas from the people who are closest to the problem. Some liberating structures my team has used are improv prototyping, 1-2-4 all, wicked questions, appreciative interviews, nine whys and wise crowds. As homework, we recommend you read through one of them each night.

Next, we'll work through two of them together; 1-2-4-all and the nine whys. Then you'll take one into your next meeting to practice. By using these liberating structures, we encourage collaboration, creativity, and buy-in.

The 1-2-4-all microstructure helps build alignment, identify solutions, and ensure everyone is on the same page. The structure is as follows:

- 1 – Everyone reflects on a challenge or question on their own for about one minute.
- 2 – Pair people up to generate ideas together for two minutes.
- 4 – Move two pairs together to exchange ideas, notice similarities and differences, and synthesize their ideas for four minutes.
- All – Bring all people back together and invite each group to share. This is when you'll be able to see you've built total alignment because everyone was part of the process.

* Note this process always works when you allow it to.

For the nine whys, it's about getting really curious and continuing to ask, "Why is that important?" nine times. By about the sixth or seventh time you ask why, you will get to the heart of the real issues.

To move past organizational roadblocks on your way to becoming an emergent culture, you'll also want to use language to your advantage. How we communicate influences how our messages are received. The words we use, as well as our body language and tone, are important. There are significant language differences between fixed and emergent companies.

Fixed companies operate with silos, turf wars, infighting, frustration, fear, and a fixed mindset where money is the main barometer. Language in fixed-mindset organizations is negative and focused on the past. Emergent companies, on the other hand, embrace collaboration, flexibility, creativity, and a growth mindset. Language is positive, future focused, and generative. Shifting from a fixed mindset to a growth mindset will support you to dismantle many of the roadblocks currently causing problems. Using language to focus on solutions and what things will look like in the future supports taking people to the place where the problem is already solved. By using future-based language, we can focus on achieving our desired outcome and take action to make it a reality, much like an athlete focuses on the finish line and not the hurdles.

You should now have a better understanding of how to dismantle roadblocks and overcome breakdowns in your organization. Take these liberating structures into your next meeting and see how they can help you find solutions and build alignment. Let's keep striving to create an emergent company culture where collaboration and a growth mindset are valued. The positive impact is pervasive!

Liberating Structures

Liberating Structures (https://www.liberatingstructures.com/) are extremely effective ways to bring decision-making and ideation to the people who are closest to the problem. Henri Lipmanowicz and Keith McCandless have done a wonderful job of creating specific exercises that tap into the collective intelligence of the team. When employees are the ones experiencing setbacks, constraints, bureaucracy, and holdups, it is extremely empowering when they are asked to solve their own problems.

These microstructures include:

One-Two-Four-All

You can immediately include everyone regardless of how large the group is. You can generate better ideas faster than ever before.

Nine Whys

With breathtaking simplicity, you can rapidly clarify for individuals and a group what is important in their work.

Wise Crowds

Wise Crowds make it possible to instantly engage a small or large group of people in helping one another.

Triz

You can clear space for innovation by helping a group let go of what it knows (but rarely admits) limits its success and by inviting creative destruction.

Appreciative Interviews

In less than one hour, a group of any size can generate the list of conditions that are essential for its success.

Wicked Questions

Wicked questions engage everyone in sharper strategic thinking by revealing entangled challenges and possibilities that are not intuitively obvious.

Where can you see it would be a good idea to bring in a liberating structure?

Closing for Leadership Teams

Congratulations on completing the section for leadership teams. You now have the tools to create a thriving team that supports innovation, engagement, and problem-solving.

Remember, it's not about whose job it is or who did what; it's about banding together to solve problems and achieve results. You've learned about the four elements of a high-performance culture and how to integrate them into your organization. We've discussed the critical role that the leadership team plays in creating and maintaining a strong and thriving team and organizational culture.

As a member of the leadership team, it's up to you to create an inspiring cause, an ultimate intent, and lead by example, ensuring that your behavior aligns with the culture you want to create. Although clear and consistent communication is a must, the words you say don't carry as much weight as what you do. If you are saying that integrity is important, but your leadership team is engaging in unethical activities, people will know that integrity is not really a value of the organization. Your actions speak louder than your words, and the actions and words of the leadership team are critically important because leaders are held to very high standards. You set the strategic direction for the organization and play a critical role in creating the structures and systems that support a healthy culture. You lead the way in all of those things.

You've also explored the importance of aligning your team with your strategy, fostering innovation and developing a strong sense of purpose and inspiring values. The role of feedback and communication in creating a culture of accountability and continuous improvement is another critical element in your organization's success.

So, take the first step as a leadership department by committing to creating an emergent, high-performance team within your organization. As you move forward, remember that creating this healthy and thriving culture is an ongoing process, not a one-time fix, and you'll need to continue to invest in the health of the human system. Keep an open mind, be receptive to feedback, and be willing to make changes when necessary. Remember, we're here to support you every step of the way.

Section 3
The Organization—Is It Ready for Breakthrough Performance?

Igniting positive, sustainable change within an organization's culture, rather than simply managing or maintaining it, is what is required to have the most influence over the effectiveness of the organization. Up to this point, you have done your personal work and worked with your team to up-level how you work with one another to begin creating an environment for higher profit, engagement, and innovation.

Good people leave companies with unhealthy cultures and that unwanted turnover has likely been like a punch in the gut. As professionals, you know that when this happens there is a serious problem. At this point in the workbook, we know you are committed to being part of the change you want to see. It is time to ignite the kind of culture where emergence is a natural occurrence. Where people are connected to the Noble Cause and experience the organization walking its talk. A culture where people feel supported and empowered to fulfill their objectives and contribute with their highest and best use of self. As with all changes, there is the possibility of change fatigue, so beware of the signs and proactively set yourself and others up to win. Keep in mind, as Deepak Chopra has said, "Every time you are tempted to react in the same old way, ask if you want to be a prisoner of the past or a pioneer of the future."

Your organization needs you to be a pioneer of the future and to support bringing the new, emergent culture forward for all those who work with you. Your efforts will serve to usher in a culture where innovation and creativity flourish, where trust and accountability are bedrock, and where great people really want to work.

The overarching theme of section 3 is to influence and catalyze people in the direction of an emergent culture. Let's dive into the areas where you can have an immediate positive influence. It will be well worth the effort!

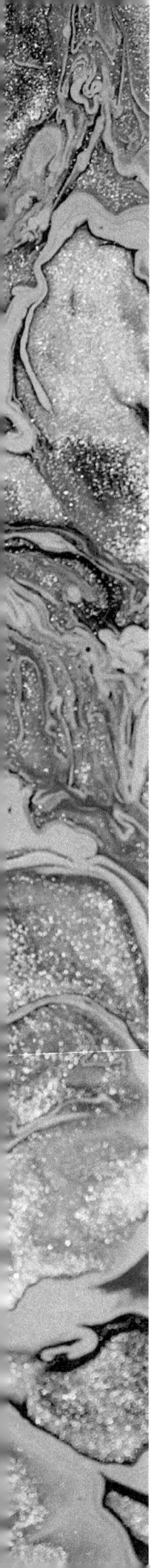

Chapter 11
The Alchemy of Enduring High Performance

Is your organization ready for breakthrough performance? The journey through change is never a smooth one. Change is a gradual and continual process that requires personal development and readiness for internal change well before making any external change. If you try to start with the external, people resist, and everything seems and probably is ten times harder. Change involves defining your WHY for the change, and what values, principles, and desired behaviors you need to support the change. Additionally, making lasting positive change requires you forecast and address any negative or harmful practices that currently exist within your workplace culture that could derail the change efforts.

In this chapter, you'll see collective intelligence as the shared beliefs, values, behaviors, and practices that emerge from a group of people interacting over time. You'll see that an emergent culture is not something that can be directly controlled or imposed; rather, it emerges naturally through the interactions, relationships, mutual understanding, and trust built within a group.

It's important to note, however, that an organization can't even begin this process until the leader as well as the leadership team have done the foundational work. Change is never-ending, and people are always growing. However, the basics of rooting out dysfunction and setting a solid foundation need to happen before delving in to transform the entire organization. You need to understand what you don't want in a culture, as much as what you do want, and you need to be able to speak about what you want in a constructive way.

When Satya Nadella was named CEO of Microsoft, he made big changes in the organization's culture. He replaced the old, aggressive behaviors of the previous leaders with calm responses and positive feedback. He made it clear that he wouldn't tolerate anger or yelling in executive meetings and instead promoted a culture of curiosity, learning, and encouragement to focus on the future. The results have been spectacular. Microsoft has become the most valuable company in the world.

Microsoft's transformation provides a tangible example of how the alchemy of healthy high-performance manifests in a human system. It requires clear values, a noble cause, and group discipline that is modeled from the top.

When leadership teams commit to inspiring and catalyzing positive organizational changes in any area required (environmental, behavioral, architectural, process and how people and talents are fully optimized), an emergent culture serves as a guiding light to direct their implementation plan. Igniting the human spirit at work leads to greater self-confidence, stronger self-awareness and deeper interconnectivity. When that happens in any environment, trust is cultivated. When people who trust one another are aligned with a noble cause, operate and interact with cohesive inspiring values, and work towards a clear vision for the future - you've got fertile ground for cooperation, teamwork and innovation. This is how leaders and the organizations they serve navigate change, and move forward with velocity.

When people are equipped, empowered and inspired to operate at their highest level, both individually and collectively, breakthroughs in performance and innovation are expected and actualized. Synchronicity, innovation, extreme ownership, and momentum are the norm within cultural alignment methodology.

Understand this is a process; it's not something that's done overnight. It can take years for this kind of change management initiative to be implemented fully, especially a culture change. Understanding the three dimensions of cultural evolution is necessary to transform an entangled, transactional, or toxic culture to a healthy, high-performance emergent culture.

- Dimension one is the Disciplines of Planned Change.
- Dimension two is about the Stages of Planned Change.
- Dimension three is about the Levels of the Human System.

Once the foundation and understanding are set, you're ready to inspire change through collective action. To create transformational change, there are eight disciplines that must be developed.

8 Disciplines of Planned Change

1. Conscious use of self – People need to bring their whole selves to the change movement, cleaning up the impact of unhealthy actions and tuning in to their unique genius.

2. Whole-systems orientation – Individuals must think as much about the big picture as themselves and understand their impact on the whole.

3. Openness to sound and current data – Everyone involved in an organizational change effort needs to understand the data supporting the change. This data could be implicit or explicit and should be both quantitative and qualitative. Data allows people involved in the change to clearly see reality and make informed decisions.

4. Constructive feedback – Both the sender and the receiver need to partner and grow in service of catalyzing positive change. All people involved in change efforts must develop a strong competency in communication.

5. Respect for collective intelligence – Individuals don't always have to be right in order to produce results. In an emergent culture, collective intelligence is always greater than the sum of its individual parts.

6. Learning from differences – Organizations need to tap into the unique genius of their people and teams to get the kind of new thinking required to change, grow, and innovate.

7. Empowerment – Change sticks when the people affected are fully empowered to solve problems and confront challenges together.

8. Support Systems – The team has resources readily available to aid them in resolving conflicts, building trust, problem solving, strengthening communication, planning, project management, etc.

Organizational transformation and change management can be precarious. We look to the five stages of planned change to scope the work, let people know what to expect and gauge success.

5 Stages of Planned Change

Contracting — Agreement within the highest level of management to specify clear goals that are consistent and aligned with the organization's noble cause and values.

Data Gathering — This is for the change-effort team to find out what is working and what is not, as well as alert and excite the organization about the coming change.

Intervening — Architecture to improve relationships, such as feedback systems, team-building events, immersion workshops, ongoing coaching, conflict management, and so on.

Evaluating — Different levels of evaluation are happening daily, weekly, and monthly—not just annually. Feedback should be continually gathered and evaluated for improvement.

Disengagement — There should be a distinguishable end, such as a closing evaluation session or a party, to celebrate this milestone, and it should create a sense of closure.

Remember, 85 percent of organizational change efforts fail because no structure existed to support and sustain the change. Don't make this mistake! Create a sustainable framework for success before you roll out your ideas and make sure the right people are fully on board and understand the goals and their role in achieving transformational change. Effective organization and communication are key.

A fundamental requirement for effective change to happen is including the right people in the change process. Diversity and inclusion is critical and expands beyond race, ethnicity and gender. It encompasses people throughout the value chain who are affected by changes being made who may have strong opinions on why change needs to happen and which solutions make sense. How might somebody in the sales team perceive inventory differently than someone in purchasing? We must bring people in with a variety of perspectives. And then finally give the power to these people to take matters in their own hands and solve the problem. In order to do that, you really have to have some framework for team empowerment.

Empowerment means giving people the power and resources to solve their own problems. It's important to provide a framework for empowerment that includes training, support, and assistance in the removal of any obstacles that may be preventing them from doing their best work. It's time to have conversations with other people in the organization committed to catalyzing positive change and discuss what that change may look like and what support is needed to make the initiative successful. Have an open dialogue about whether people are really interested in doing the work, because if they're not, it'll fail.

We had a client named Miguel, and before he really understood what empowerment was, he would say, "Magi, they're empowered. I promoted them." Miguel was not looking deeply enough. Have you trained them? Have you found out what's in their way that might be keeping them from doing a better job? He just didn't understand because Miguel's always felt empowered. He never needed anybody to empower him. He had innate empowerment, but that's not the case for people who are not executives. He thought he was empowering them, but he wasn't. In some cases he actually promoted people to their highest level of incompetence, which is common, because when you like somebody, they seem capable in one area, and you think it translates to all areas.

There are various stages of change management, such as awareness, preparation, implementation, and sustainability. Each stage involves different challenges and requires different skills and strategies to overcome them. Change doesn't happen overnight.

One important aspect of personal development during a culture change or any change initiative is developing self-awareness and the ability to see the whole system. This means recognizing how our actions and decisions impact others both upstream and downstream, and not just solving for our own experience. Whole-system thinking is essential for building a culture or making changes that impact the whole organization. For any type of change to work it must be inclusive, collaborative, and sustainable.

To nurture a healthy, intentional and high-performance organizational culture, we also need to collect and use sound and current data. This data aids us in identifying areas that are not working or not working as well as they could be, and moving towards making improvements in the system that are more aligned with organizations' Noble Cause, values, and goals. We also need to be able to communicate the data in a constructive way that focuses on what is missing and what can be improved, rather than just pointing out what is wrong.

In order to create successful organizational change initiatives, you need to follow a series of steps, including defining your values and desired behaviors, identifying areas of improvement, creating a plan for change, implementing the plan, and measuring and sustaining the change over time. Despite best efforts, transformational initiatives fail 85 percent of the time. To prevent this, we recommend our clients utilize a change management check list and embed that into the overall plan for change. It is important to remember that no change is easy and that challenges, roadblocks and obstacles will happen. The question is, are you prepared to navigate them when they do occur.

Fostering an emergent culture that delivers high performance is a continuous process of growth and improvement. By following the steps outlined in this chapter and being mindful of the challenges and opportunities that come with change, we can continue to cultivate a human system that is more aligned with our values and goals, and that supports the success of our organization and its members.

Ultimately, it is important to nurture a culture of trust and transparency, where everyone feels comfortable speaking up and sharing their ideas and concerns. This requires fostering an environment where communication is open and honest and where everyone feels that their voice is heard and valued. It is also important to cultivate a growth mindset and a willingness to take risks and try new things. This requires creating an environment where mistakes are seen as opportunities for learning and growth rather than something to be punished or avoided.

Overall, the alchemy of high performance involves creating a Environment that encourages and supports mastery, fosters a sense of ownership and accountability, and cultivates a growth mindset and a culture of trust and transparency. It requires ongoing commitment and effort, but the rewards can be tremendous in terms of organizational success and employee satisfaction. Let's dig into some processes that can help!

How Do We Make Change Happen?

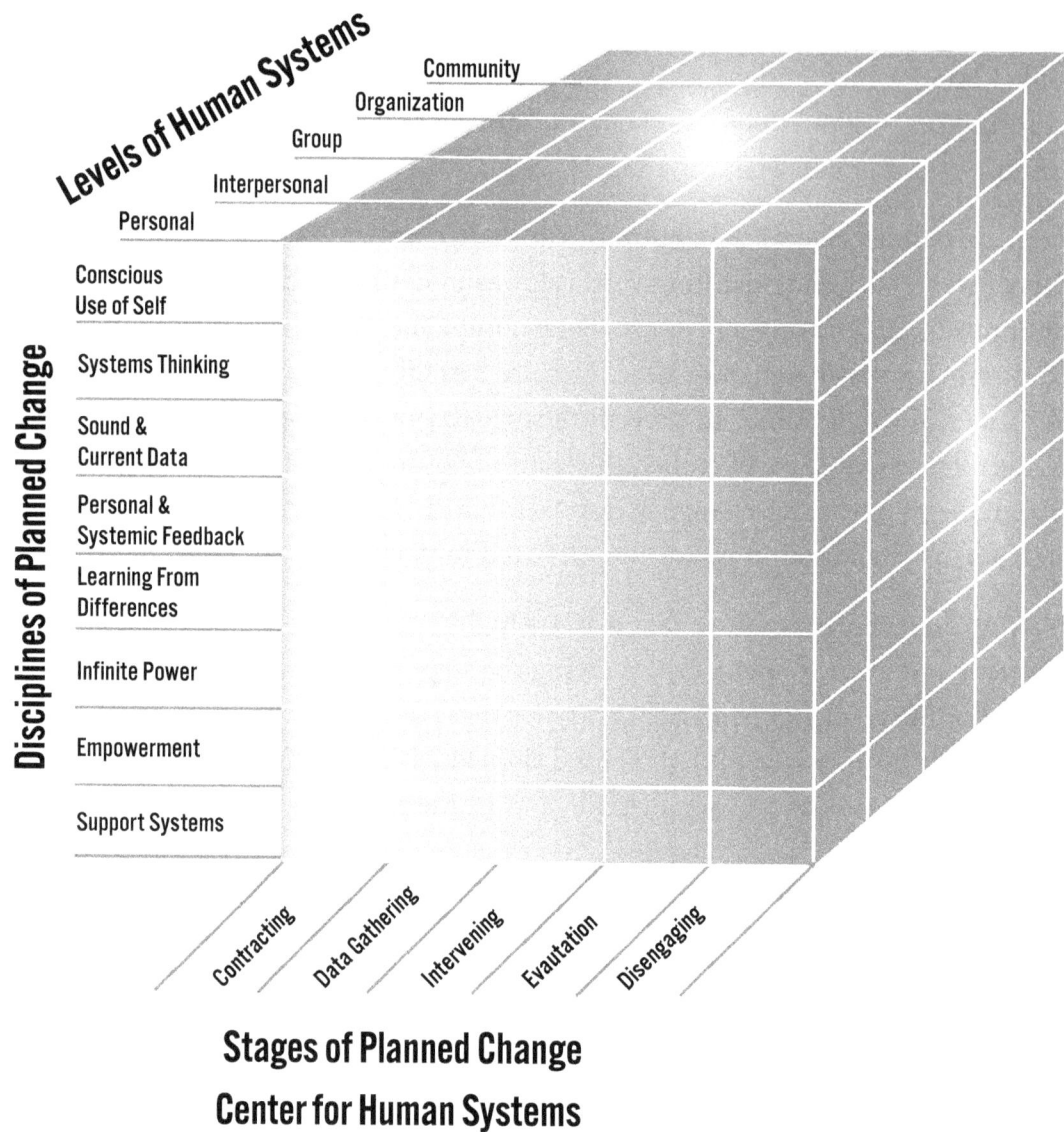

Levels of Human Systems

Community
Organization
Group
Interpersonal
Personal

Disciplines of Planned Change

Conscious Use of Self

Systems Thinking

Sound & Current Data

Personal & Systemic Feedback

Learning From Differences

Infinite Power

Empowerment

Support Systems

Contracting Data Gathering Intervening Evauation Disengaging

Stages of Planned Change
Center for Human Systems

Change takes time, recurrence of behaviors, habits, and actions, and the right environment that enriches and stimulates enthusiasm for change—the energy must be above the power and freedom line and the mood must be courageous or better.

There are five levels of human systems, beginning with the personal and moving up to the overall community, which includes all your stakeholders (customers, investors, vendors, partners, and such).

There are eight disciplines required to lead effective change — Oxford defines disciplines as: train oneself to do something in a controlled and habitual way.

There are five stages of planned change—steps and phases that a group must experience to ideate, initiate, implement, and sustain change.

On a scale of one to ten, how does your team rate on the Disciplines? How can these disciplines help you move through change with positive and effective results?

Conscious Use of Self	Team members are skilled in self awareness internally and externally	
Systems Thinking	Thinking looks at people, production, and the organization overall when ideating and making decisions	
Sound & Current Data	Team members appreciate and utilize relevant data when identifying organizational challenges and problems and ideating solutions	
Personal & Systemic Feedback	Team members are open to hearing feedback even if the perspectives they are hearing are different or in contrast to what they already think	
Learning From Differences	Team members appreciate others who see things differently or from different point of views, there is a willingness to listen, hear, and respond in a way that makes people feel appreciated and valued regardless if you implement their ideas	
Infinite Power	Team members understand and are eager to tap into the collective intelligence of the whole	
Empowerment	Team member experience autonomy, freedom, and creativity in how they make change happen and get work done	
Support Systems	There are systems, training, and resources in place that give change agents and team members what they need, how they need it, and when they need it so they feel and experience being supported in the new work coming from making change	

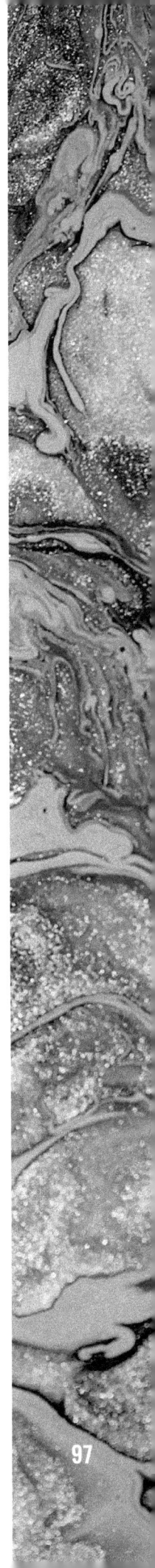

What Is an Emergent Culture?

An emergent culture is a culture where people assemble, affiliate, and innovate regularly. The trust is high and the willingness to give up control and put ego aside is high. The bottom line is that exceptional teamwork and unrivaled innovation is a result of bringing people together who are capable, competent, and intrinsically motivated in their role and to the overall noble cause. When all these pieces are in place, your team is set up and ready to not only meet the moment, but to anticipate and be in the moment.

Definition of Emergence

In philosophy, systems theory, science, and art, emergence occurs when a complex entity has properties or behaviors that its parts do not have on their own and emerge only when they interact in a wider whole. Emergence plays a central role in theories of integrative levels and of complex systems.

List the systems, teams, processes and circumstances in your organization that need change efforts.

Describe the situation, why it is a problem for the company, and the impact on the organization from a financial, human system, customer experience, and organizational effectiveness perspective.

List the people most impacted by the problem and what strengths they bring to a collaborative ideation session.

Create the narrative of what you will say to them to enroll them in being part of the positive change effort.

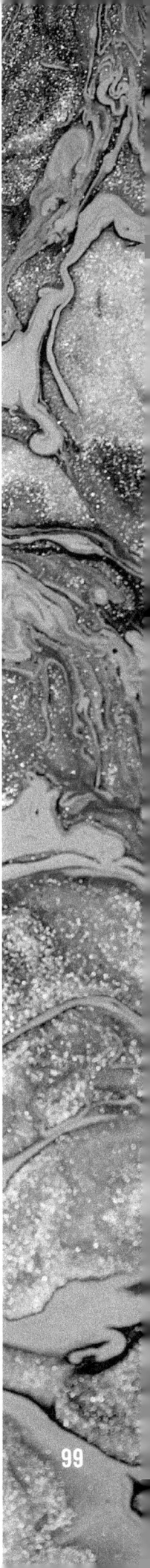

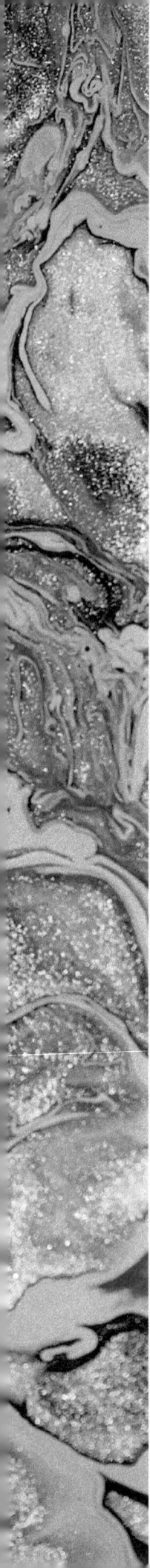

Chapter 12
Getting to Critical Mass

When a behavior or idea reaches critical mass, it becomes ingrained in the culture and is more likely to be accepted and adopted by the team. This can be especially important when trying to implement a new culture, change an existing culture or usher in a new way of working together to get things done. To achieve critical mass, you'll need to get about 10 percent of your people to be willing to take on the tasks of being a catalyst or agent of change—and not just giving lip service, but truly evangelizing the desired change.

To start, let's define critical mass. Simply put, critical mass refers to the point at which a certain behavior or idea becomes self-sustaining and spreads rapidly throughout a group or community. Why is critical mass so important in building a successful culture or leading a change that requires the culture to shift how they work to accomplish goals? When you kick off a change initiative, we recommend a launch event. Just after the inspiring communication about the change has been delivered, it's time to get at least 10 percent of the people in the organization to be your partners. The goal of the launch event is to get people behind the vision, let them really see their place in it, and demonstrate that the change initiative is fully embraced at the highest levels of the organization. If successful, people will begin moving in the right direction. It sends a positive message to everyone. It's a chance to talk about what it's going to take to really alter how things get done and ask who is in. You'll let them know that "in" means they're going to spend 10 percent of their working hours doing this, which means they might have to give some discretionary contribution. They might be working on things on weekends, evenings, or early in the morning, but the payoff is amazing because they will get to be instrumental in catalyzing positive systemic change that elevates the organization and those who work in it. In this inspired setting, the first volunteers typically step forward.

Below is the framework for facilitating that initial meeting to speak about the changes you are planning and how you need people to work together and nurture the right conditions for positive change to take place. It is important to inspire people towards the future and enroll them in the possibilities, while also telling the truth about the uphill climb that is required. Then you'll invite people who really want to be part of the future of the organization and part of this change, to step up. Once you have volunteers it is important to have a selection process for who will own which elements of the change initiative. Will is very important during change efforts and so is skill, availability and time commitment. You'll need someone to lead that team, so you have to

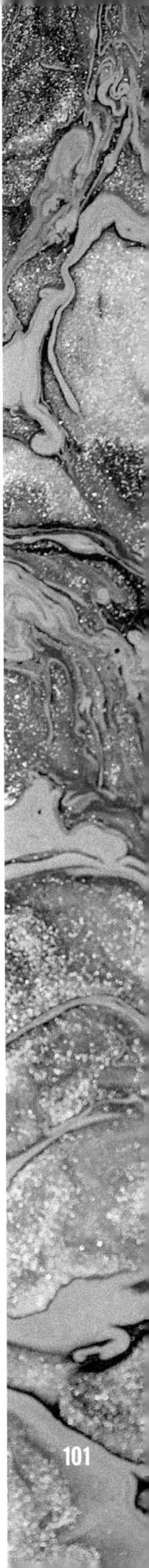

find out who in your organization would be best suited to do that, and then you have to determine if you need the help of an interventionist or a culture coach.

Next, we'll talk about the ideal-actual culture inventory, where you'll survey the people in your organization by geography, division, department, longevity, and seniority and ask them what they want in an ideal culture. About 2 weeks later, you'll ask them in a separate survey what they think of the current culture. In the alchemy of high performance, a healthy culture requires four things:

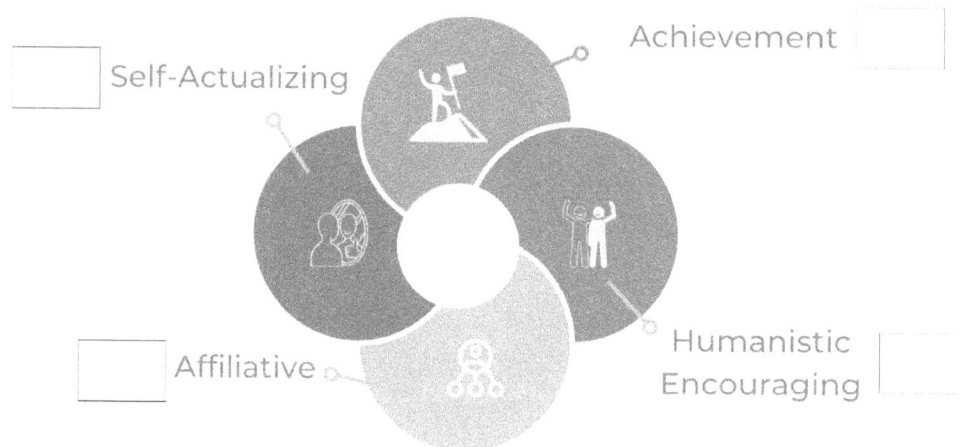

4 Core Needs of Emergent Culture
Satisfaction needs

Rate the following needs on a scale from 1 to 10, with 10 being the highest and 1 being the lowest. Write your answer in the blank provided.

Self-Actualizing

Achievement

Affiliative

Humanistic Encouraging

Rate your team on how competent it is at delivering on the core needs of a healthy, intentional high-performance culture. (scale 1-10)

1. It's a self-actualizing culture where people experience themselves as living their highest use of self and they're actually experiencing fulfillment on the job.

2. It's an achievement-oriented culture where results are not only important, they're measured, and people are held to that standard of results.

3. It's humanistic, where you care about people and understand what's important to them. You care about what they're doing in their life and that they're okay. And you've got that built into your culture, not just at the CEO level but with every manager.

4. It's a culture where people are affiliating. They're collaborating and working together to solve problems and invent solutions. This is where you can really leverage liberating structures.

When you do an ideal-culture survey, 90 percent of the people respond that they desire to work in an environment that is congruent with what we are referring to as an Emergent Culture. While some people think extreme behaviors are the only way to get things done or to make it through the day, the majority of people do not. Healthy people want to work in healthy, intentional, and high-performance environments.

So the next step in the survey is to look at the current culture. Typically, it's either somewhat entangled, transactional, or toxic. With an entangled culture, you have polarization. You have people who are super aggressive, competitive, oppositional, and perfectionistic or who like to power up over people. Within a transactional culture, people are passive, compliant, and conforming. They ask for permission and are very complacent. They do what they're asked but nothing else. They do only what is asked and actually beleive they're working hard. These diligent doers are mostly not aware they could be doing more, and taking more initiative. With this type of polarity, you often have a transactional, or gridlocked organizational culture where it is very difficult, stressful and time consuming to make systemic change (even when it is for the better).

When the polarities between passive and aggressive are extreme, it is a breeding ground for toxicity.

Regardless of if your ideal/actual culture assessment results reveal you have a defensive aggressive or passive aggressive (or both) culture, it's important to learn from the polarities.

Once you understand the contrast between what people want and what they perceive they are experiencing, it becomes easy to see where work needs to be done to bridge the gap. It is crucial that you address the people side of the house BEFORE pushing change through. If you don't, the resistance you will encounter will be unmanageable, thwart your plans, and cost you incredible sums of money and employee engagement.

It's important to be aware of your team's response to the survey results. For instance, when I worked with one company, I gave them a survey and they found out that 60 percent of the workforce felt that they had an entangled culture. The employees felt that the managers and executives were in the way of change. This was hard for the executives and managers to take.

If this sounds like your company, you need to change the mindset of your executives and managers. When you conduct a survey, you might find that some people are unwilling to hear the results. When this happens, it's important to coach them and help them understand how important cross departmental employee buy-in and cooperation is to the achievement of change initiatives and goals.

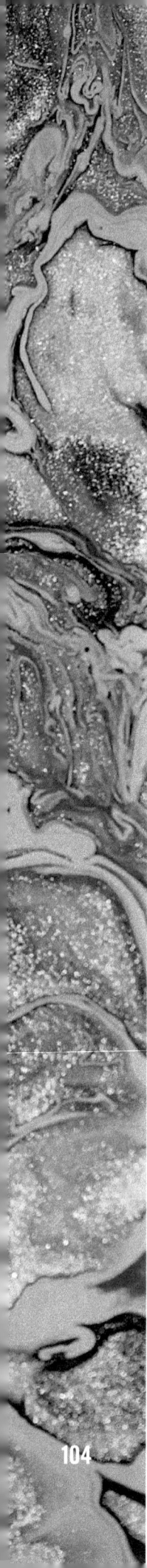

HOW CULTURE WORKS

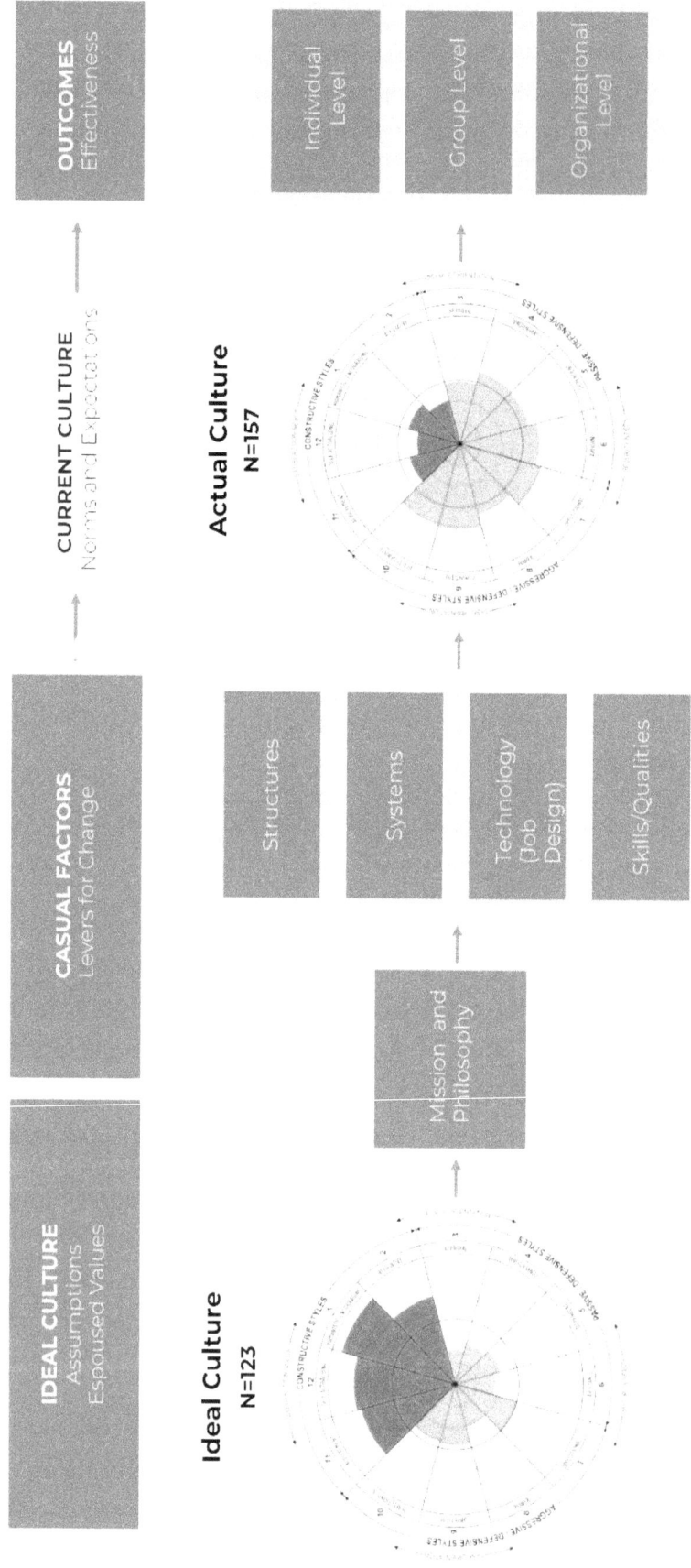

IDEAL CULTURE
Assumptions
Espoused Values

CASUAL FACTORS
Levers for Change

CURRENT CULTURE
Norms and Expectations

OUTCOMES
Effectiveness

Structures

Systems

Technology
(Job
Design)

Skills/Qualities

Mission and
Philosophy

Individual
Level

Group Level

Organizational
Level

Ideal Culture
N=123

Actual Culture
N=157

BARCHART OF CAUSAL FACTORS

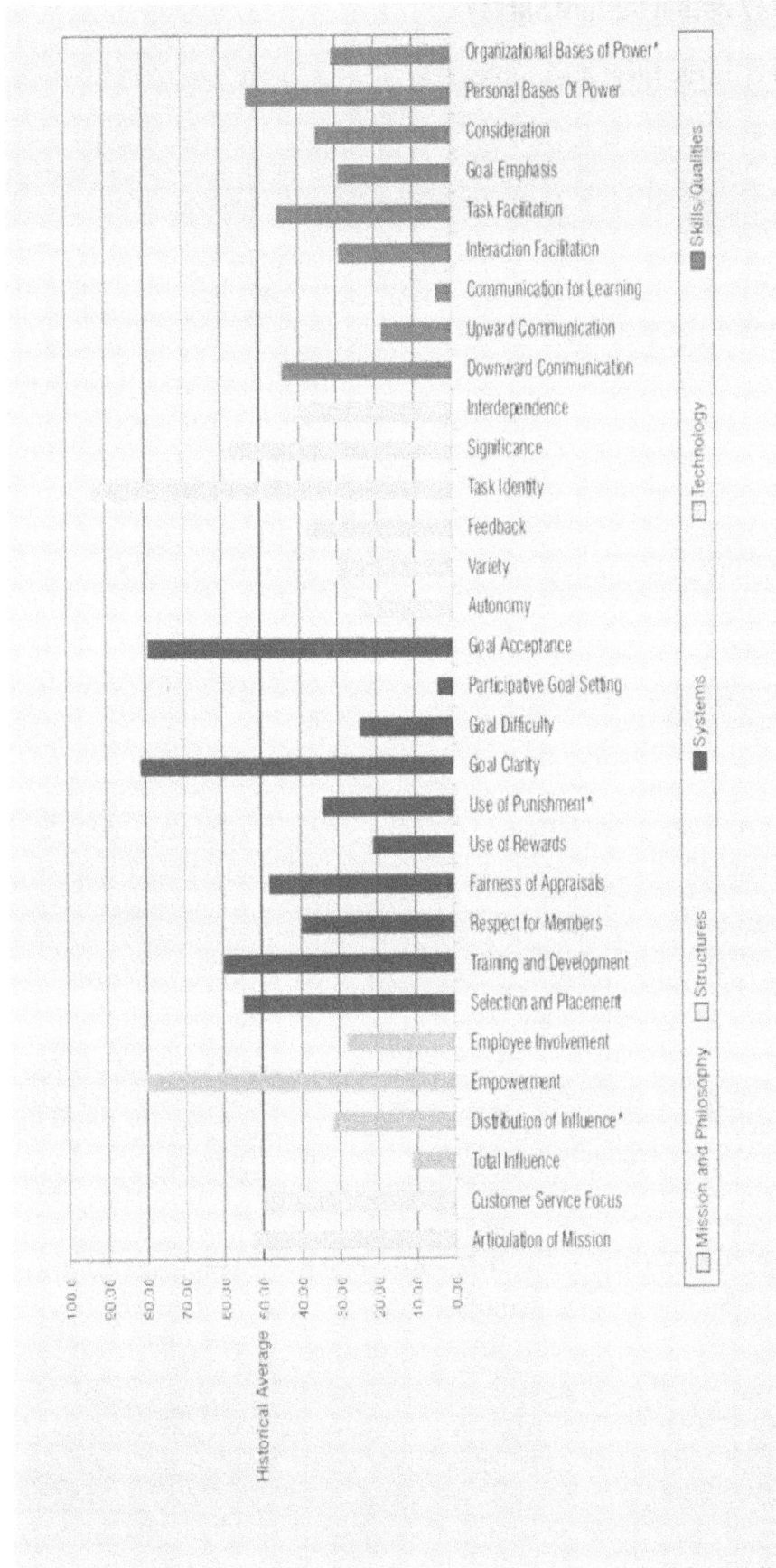

Organizational Bases of Power*
Personal Bases Of Power
Consideration
Goal Emphasis
Task Facilitation
Interaction Facilitation
Communication for Learning
Upward Communication
Downward Communication
Interdependence
Significance
Task Identity
Feedback
Variety
Autonomy
Goal Acceptance
Participative Goal Setting
Goal Difficulty
Goal Clarity
Use of Punishment*
Use of Rewards
Fairness of Appraisals
Respect for Members
Training and Development
Selection and Placement
Employee Involvement
Empowerment
Distribution of Influence*
Total Influence
Customer Service Focus
Articulation of Mission

■ Skills-Qualities
□ Technology
■ Systems
□ Structures
□ Mission and Philosophy

100.00 90.00 80.00 70.00 60.00 50.00 40.00 30.00 20.00 10.00 0.00

Historical Average

Ideal / Actual Culture Survey

Review the **ideal** circumplex.

Review the **actual** circumplex.

What is apparent to you?

Take a look at the causal factors.

From looking at the data, what assessments can you make? Write down your thoughts and create a narrative.

What do you notice is in the company's way? Write down your thoughts and create a narrative.

Based on what you have learned so far, what basic recommendations can you make for this company to move closer to the ideal? Write down your thoughts and create a narrative.

What specific conversations for action do you want to have? Write down your thoughts and create a narrative.

Communication is Key for Alignment
Evaluate Clear Concise Communication

Where is communication breaking down in your organization?

What do you see that could make the needed differences?

What you have learned about EXAMPLE X company, and how does that reflect your organization?

If a professionally administered Culture Assessment is out of reach, you can opt in to take KeenAlignments' FREE organizational culture assessment. Visit KeenAlignment. com and click take the FREE culture assessment.

Getting to critical mass is all about optimizing the collective genius in the human system, and the ideal-actual culture inventory aides you in understanding what is working and what needs attention. It's about getting the right people engaged in the efforts and making changes that positively impact the organization and the people in it. Critical mass can sometimes be difficult to predict or control. While there are certain strategies that can be used to increase the likelihood of reaching critical mass, ultimately it's up to the group or community to decide whether to adopt a particular idea or behavior.

As you work to cultivate an environment that thrives in the face of change, remember the importance of critical mass. By identifying key influencers and working to cultivate cohesive, productive behaviors that foster trust and cooperation, you increase the likelihood of inspiring a human system where people are intrinsically motivated, engaging in exceptional teamwork and generating unrivaled innovation – all in service of fulfilling on your Noble Cause. Let's get the influencers involved!

Who are your 10 percent?

How would you define a culture catalyst?

Who are the people you experience as being willing to be key members of and part of the change?

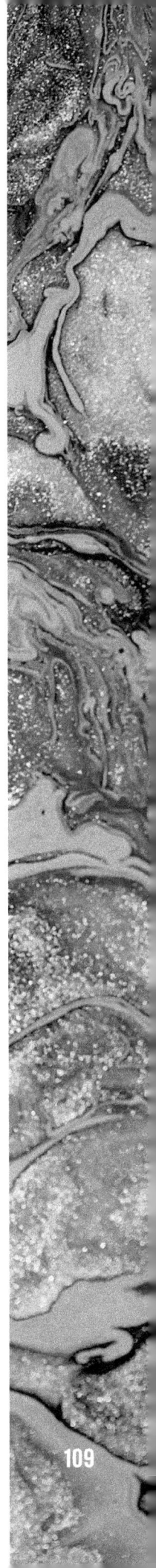

Stage	Actions Needed	Pitfalls
Establish a sense of urgency	• Examine market and competitive realities for potential crises and untapped opportunities. • Convince at least 75% of your managers that the status quo is more dangerous than the unknown.	• Underestimating the difficulty of driving people from their comfort zones • Becoming paralyzed by risks
Form a powerful guiding coalition	• Assemble a group with shared commitment and enough power to lead the change effort. • Encourage them to work as a team outside the normal hierarchy.	• No prior experience in teamwork at the top • Relegating team leadership to an HR, quality, or strategic planning executive rather than a senior line manager
Create a vision	• Create a vision to direct the change effort. • Develop strategies for realizing that vision.	• Presenting a vision that's too complicated or vague to be communicated in five minutes
Communicate the vision	• Use every vehicle possible to communicate the new vision and strategies for achieving it. • Teach new behaviors by the example of the guiding coalition.	• Under communicating the vision • Behaving in ways antithetical to the vision
Empower others to act on the vision	• Remove or alter systems or structures undermining the vision. • Encourage risk taking and nontraditional ideas, activities, and actions.	• Failing to remove powerful individuals who resist the change effort
Plan for and create short-term wins	• Define and engineer visible performance improvements. • Recognize and reward employees contributing to those improvements.	• Leaving short-term successes up to chance • Failing to score successes early enough (12-24 months into the change effort)
Consolidate improvements and produce more change	• Use increased credibility from early wins to change systems, structures, and policies undermining the vision. • Hire, promote, and develop employees who can implement the vision. • Reinvigorate the change process with new projects and change agents.	• Declaring victory too soon—with the first performance improvement • Allowing resistors to convince "troops" that the war has been won
Institutionalize new approaches	• Articulate connections between new behaviors and corporate success. • Create leadership development and succession plans consistent with the new approach.	• Not creating new social norms and shared values consistent with changes • Promoting people into leadership positions who don't personify the new approach

Chapter 13

Aligning the Collective Intelligence of a Human System

Chapter 13 explores the topic of aligning the collective intelligence of a human system. The seven levels of individual and organizational effectiveness are critical for understanding the power of energy on a human system.

BEabove Leadership, with source material from Consciousness Mapped from Dave Hawkins, has identified seven major energetic fields of personal, group, and organizational effectiveness. These levels offer an excellent barometer for people to become aware of where they are operating at and if desired, what to do to move up a level.

Seven Levels of Personal, Group & Organizational Effectiveness

EFFECTIVE	7	Synchronicity
	6	Innovation
	5	Engagement
	4	Courage
		Power and Freedom
INEFFECTIVE	3	Frustration
	2	Fear
	1	Hopelessness

- Synchronicity – Working from a true understanding that what is within creates what is outside; focusing on creating a positive experience for all; the ability to see the gift and possibility in anything.
- Innovation – Ability to set aside ego, personal agendas, and perceived restrictions and explore possibilities from all angles; the quest for and focus on the most effective solution to the problem or goal.
- Engagement – Desire to bring value, to be a contributor; basic enjoyment of the enterprise; focus on assets and strengths rather than limitations and detriments.
- Courage – Willingness to take a stand against previously held negative or disempowering beliefs and actions, trusting in the possibility of a positive future (often despite current evidence that a positive future is not likely or predictable).

- Frustration – Focus on fighting and jockeying for position against (not with) others; the feeling that the external world (people and circumstances) must be resisted.
- Fear – Belief that one must protect against almost certain loss, attack, or disappointment.
- Hopelessness – A fundamental inability to see or work toward a positive future.

Each field of effectiveness drives behavior, communication, and perceptions. The power of energy on a human system cannot be overstated, and its energy has a significant impact on the individuals within that system. This is how good people get burned out at lower levels. The mismatch in energy is not sustainable. Neuroscience experts, behavioral scientists, and cultural anthropologists believe that it is only organizations calibrating at level four (courage) or above that have the ability to focus on rational, thoughtful analysis.

According to Michael Broom, who was quoted in the *Ignite Culture* book, a human system can be thought of as a Rubik's Cube (see page 96), consisting of eleven elements that work together to determine the health of the system. Its health, in turn, determines whether an emergent culture can develop, where exceptional teamwork and intrinsic motivation lead to new ideas that deliver on the Noble Cause. The health of the organization is greatly impacted by which level the human system is operating at. Trust, mutual understanding, transparency, communication, respect and accountability are all behaviors that impact the energy of the environment.

These characteristics of human systems deserve attention because they help clarify what is needed as you navigate cultural transformation.

1. Goal achievement is the primary purpose of any system. Clarity is paramount for effectiveness.

2. Alignment of system members is a primary strategy for goal achievement that, without alignment, tends to take the form of suppression of differences (conformity) or other win/lose power dynamics (power struggles, turf battles) rather than collaborative, win/win synergetic dynamics.

3. Feedback loops regulate the behavior of systems and keep the system on target toward its goals. Performance data, rewards, penalties, and permissions are examples of feedback.

4. The effectiveness of human systems over time is proportional to the quality of the relationships within the system. Trust and mutual understanding are indicators of high-quality relationships.

5. A problematic human system will mitigate the effectiveness of related human, mechanical, or electronic systems. Failure to frequently attend to the quality of a human system is costly in terms of effectiveness and efficiency.

6. For a system to be doing what it's doing, everyone in that system must be doing what they're doing. Accordingly, responsibility is always mutual—everyone is to be credited, and everyone is to be blamed. Everyone impacts the system, and the system impacts everyone.

7. Any member of a system will consistently succeed (or fail) only with the support of the system.

8. The behavior of leaders (as collectively interpreted by followers) has a significant impact on the behavior (collaboration, competition, conformity, anarchy) that occurs within human systems.

9. The members of systems are diverse. Innovation is dependent on the effective use of diversity. At the same time, the preponderance of problematic human systems stems from differences (diversity) being squashed into conformity or used for hostility and contention.

10. Human-system problems are often better dealt with through improving relationships (trust and mutual understanding) among the system's members rather than removing/replacing members. This requires being curious about what's going on rather than judging those involved. After all, you too are a part of that system.

11. Managing change in human systems requires seeing ourselves as part of the system, understanding our impact on the system at hand, and modifying our behavior as needed.

How the human system works together inside of trust determines its health. And it's the health of that human system that determines if you will ever get to an emergent culture where there's exceptional teamwork and where everybody's bringing their intrinsic motivation to create new ideas, processes, and innovation that serve as conduits to fulfill the noble cause.

To work within your small group, there is a checklist of sixteen elements to consider. By ranking these elements on a scale of one to ten, you can get a clear picture of your system's effectiveness. The health of a human system is critical in determining whether we can achieve an emergent culture where there's exceptional teamwork and everyone brings their intrinsic motivation.

Small groups are an effective way to ignite this change quickly. We can achieve this by getting the 10 percent to evangelize with small groups. So, in a thousand-person company, for example, you can have a hundred change agents meeting with five people at a time, which helps critical mass. By bringing in liberating structures, you ensure that everyone's voice is heard, and a wide array of perspectives and inputs are brought to the group.

In summary, this chapter covers the seven levels of individual or organizational effectiveness, the definition of a human system, a checklist for assessing the health of your group, and the importance of small groups in igniting change. We believe this information serves you in aligning the collective intelligence of your human system and promotes a culture of exceptional teamwork and innovation. These practical tips ignite positive, enduring change in your organization.

A Checklist for Highly Productive Teams

The effectiveness of a team as a human system precedes sustainable and effective task accomplishment.

- ☐ Are outcomes, goals, strategies, roles, values, and action steps clear to all team members?

- ☐ Are goals for team effectiveness clear as well?

- ☐ Are the members of the team interdependent on one another for the successful accomplishment of the team's goals?

- ☐ Do team members see themselves as a team?

- ☐ Does each member feel ownership for the success of the team?

- ☐ Have team members contracted to consistently and proactively help and support one another and not allow members to fail?

- ☐ Are the goals of each individual member known and supported as well as team goals?

- ☐ Have high-quality relationships been established among all members?

- ☐ Does the team have the diversity needed to accomplish its goals?

- ☐ Is the diversity on the team used for learning and innovation rather than wasteful contention and conformity?

- ☐ Is curiosity the primary means of dealing with and exploring differences? Or are differences a trigger for establishing who's right and who's wrong (winners and losers)?

☐ Do team members feel empowered enough to speak effectively regarding ways to improve the team's effectiveness?

☐ Is team-based dialogic feedback routinely used to maintain the team and check its members remain on course?

☐ Do team members believe their leader(s), formal or informal, genuinely care—through expressing interest, curiosity, and appreciation—about them and the team?

☐ Is the team as a whole rewarded for high performance?

☐ Are team members held accountable for keeping agreements that have been made? What are the consequences for consistently keeping agreements, and what are the consequences for consistently not keeping agreements?

What have you learned about the seven levels?

In your own words, how would you describe each level and where do you see these levels showing up at work?

What ideas do you have for how you can move yourself from one level to the next? (If you are stopped in this area, the Master Class has many exercises and spot learnings in the Response Agility modules.)

How can you support your team members in recognizing where they are and in moving up to the next level?

Introduce the seven levels to five to eight members of your team and ask where they are at and why they feel they are there.

Where do they think they are?

Why?

Chapter 14

The Transformative Energy of a Self-Actualized Culture

We believe you are now much closer to understanding what is needed to lead an emergent, self-actualized culture. This chapter discusses the transformative energy of such a culture and how to achieve it. We'll explore the emergent culture model, which highlights the three key components of a self-actualized culture: noble cause, inspiring values, and unique talents that operate in sync to create exceptional teamwork, intrinsic motivation, and unrivaled innovation. We'll also examine the architecture and structure that optimizes the genius of your people and transforms your organization into a thriving and successful entity. There's much to discuss, so let's get to it.

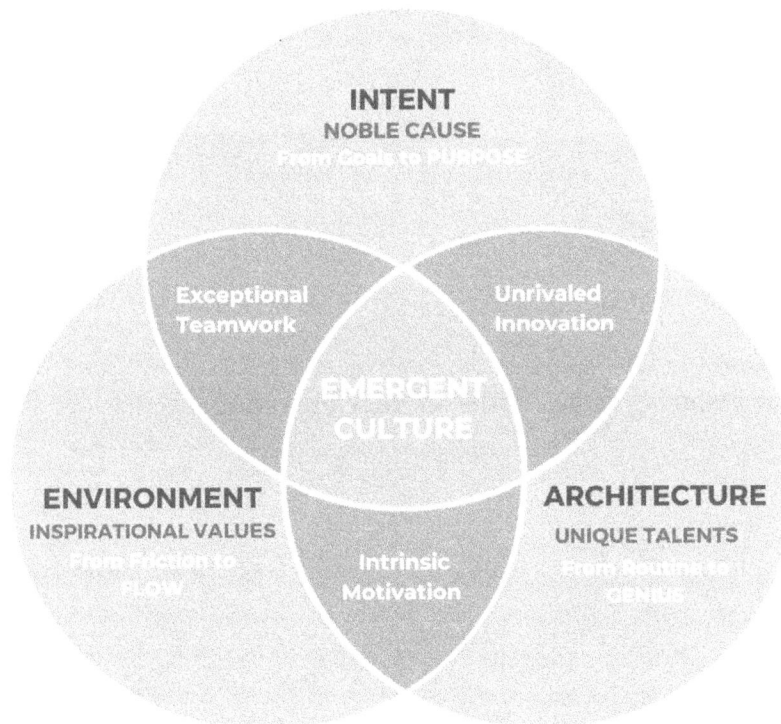

Intent

What is the Organization's reason for being?

How do you serve and contribute to your customers, to society, and to the world?

What changes are needed to enable the organization to achieve its overall intention or goal?

Environment:

What are your inspiring values? How are they operationalized?

What behaviors does your organization expect, develop, and reward?

What specific training does your organization offer to empower and enable employees to operate congruently with the inspiring values and the required behaviors?

Architecture:

What structure or systems does the organization offer to elevate the human experience at work?

What do people need to feel supported? How does your organization cultivate individual and collective genius in your human system?

What kinds of communication, interactions, and/or meetings are you leveraging for eliminating VUCA and keeping people in the know about your progress?

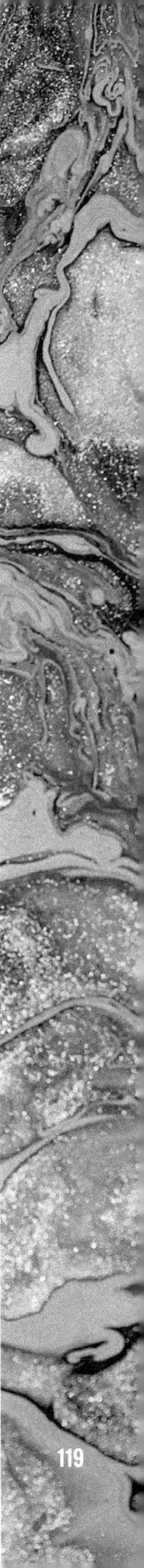

What support would make the biggest difference? Where do people need support? What kind of support will make the biggest difference? How do you know?

What are the rewards for operating in alignment with the organization's noble cause, inspirational values, and ideal culture behaviors (achievement, self-actualization, affiliation, humanistic)? What are the consequences for not?

To start, let's acknowledge the great resignation of 2021, which started in response to a global pandemic. This shift in the workforce seems to be here to stay. It reflects a deep dissatisfaction with the old, outmoded, command and control organizations. Employees are unfulfilled and unhappy. It is not the healthy, intentional and high-performance organizations that people are leaving. It is the workplaces that do not emphasize the importance of fostering an environment where trust, mutual understanding, respect and teamwork is just as important as goals, accountability, achievement and results.

The Emergent Culture model pictorializes that when you inspire your people to align around a Noble Cause they believe in, you empower them to contribute as often as possible at their level of individual and collective genius and you redirect divergent objectives, agendas and behaviors, to inspiring values and behaviors that shape a healthy, intentional high-performance environment. Here you gain three benefits: intrinsic motivation from the people in the human system, exceptional teamwork both intra and interdepartmental and unrivaled innovation. These three positive outcomes act as rocket fuel for organizational performance. Without a noble cause, people churn out work, but don't experience passion in what they do. Without alignment around inspiring values and healthy organizational behaviors, there is no integrity in how people operate and treat each other. Without people's intrinsic motivation and a desire to create solutions together, there is no evolution.

To cultivate a human system where high achievement and self-actualization is possible it requires a purpose big enough and powerful enough for people to connect to at a visceral level. The overarching intent needs to be a cause that people can feel good about investing their time, attention and effort in. The environment in which people work and operate in must be an environment that stimulates above the line energy, where leaders and those who follow, walk the talk consistent with the espoused values. When values are not honored or respected, the organization needs to have consequences in place to redirect poor behavior and maintain the integrity of the values. If this does not happen, trust will be lost, and once that happens it takes tremendous effort to rebuild. To elevate people's contribution from routine to genius, you need the right type of architecture in place. Systems, processes, and structures (not too much) that best utilizes people's time, cuts through constraints and liberates how people work together, share ideas and innovate. Think about Architecture as the framework that brings out the best in people. Framework includes how the organization develops its strategy, how new people are hired and onboarded, how people are selected and trained for Management roles, and how change is catalyzed, lead, implemented and sustained. This even includes how meetings are run, the type of meetings, how long the meetings are, who is in meetings, etc. Most organizational breakdowns occur because of a lack of planning around how projects or initiatives will move forward. Consider architecture the blueprint for achieving breakthrough success.

This chapter highlights the architecture needed to bring the right people into the company and optimize their genius. We'll provide a checklist for attracting and recruiting the right people, onboarding them in a way that exemplifies the noble cause and environment you want to build, training them, growing them, rewarding them, recognizing them, promoting them, and retaining them. All of these fundamentals need to be a part of the architecture to optimize the genius of your people.

Building this architecture is easier said than done. Most companies have a process for hiring and firing, and they might have a process for learning and development. However most companies lack the architecture needed to create the environment they want. This section provides guidance on building that architecture.

We also discuss gridlock and how to sniff it out. Signs of gridlock include infighting, nitpicking, avoidance of responsibility, sidetracking, and gossiping. These are all things that hold individuals, teams and organizations back. All of these behaviors are below the power and freedom line in the seven levels, where frustration, fear, and hopelessness reside.

Culture Is Energy

Every organism in the universe is emitting energy. Every person emits energy. Every organization is an organism and emits energy. The seven levels is a highly effective barometer for your company's energy. We encourage you to socialize the Seven levels with individual and teams. This has been a very effective way to take the pulse on people. One way to use the levels is at the beginning of a meeting. When the meeting leader gives people an opportunity to check-in on how they are doing, even if only for a few minutes, meetings flow much more smoothly. When people have an opportunity to say what is on their mind they can "name it, to tame it" and get back to the agenda for the meeting. You will also find that people remember much more from the meeting and are more engaged in the subject at hand. The more familiar people in the workplace are with the Seven Levels, the more the Seven levels can support them in recognizing what is happening with themselves. Self-Awareness is key to knowing when one needs to recalibrate and self-regulate. This is a fundamental in an emergent culture. When each individual on a team understands how to recalibrate, then the team can do this as a collective.

To summarize, this chapter covers the transformative energy of a self-actualized culture and how to optimize the genius of your people through the right architecture and structure.

Architecture for the Human System

List the stages of your employee life cycle that are clear and defined as well as deliver experience to the employee (for better or worse).

What parts or stages of your employee life cycle are aligned with your noble cause? Your mission? Your values?

What specific behaviors and actions does your company reward?

What are the prerequisites for considering candidates for management roles?

What is the method that your company utilizes to develop next-level leaders and new managers and leaders?

Next level

New managers

Leaders

How can you deploy liberating structures in your leadership development?

What needs to happen to ensure communication is consistent, clear, and concise, and that top-level thoughts and messaging get into the hearts and heads of your employees?

What could your organization achieve if you unleashed the positive energy of individuals, teams and the collective?

What commitments are you willing to make to cultivate or continue to foster a healthy, intentional and high-performance organizational culture?

It is important to remember that all living organisms, including organizations, are biological systems.

Organisms are biological entries. Nature is biological. Human beings are biological. Human systems are biological organisms. Organizations are organisms. So, it is understandable that we want to apply principles of nature in teaching how organizations remain strong.

In nature, the only way an organism can continue to survive is by having the right environment to evolve or it becomes extinct. In an organization, the right environment is what culture is all about. This "right environment" fosters the type of energy that is fertile ground for growth, development, and evolution of individuals, teams and the collective.

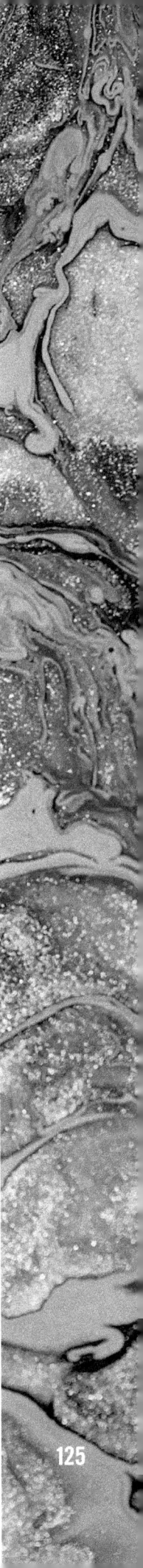

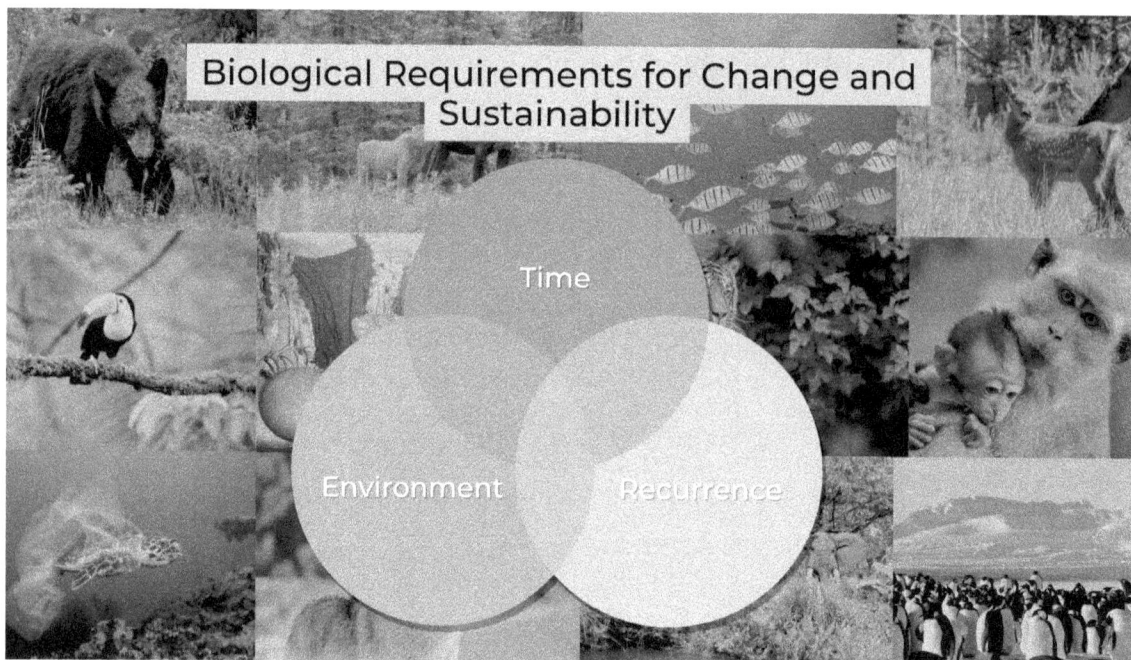

Biological Requirements for Change and Sustainability

Time

Environment   Recurrence

The Autonomy Course

Any organism must evolve over time. As the world changes and as circumstances change, every biological entity needs time evolve (This goes for a new employee, a new team, a new leader, or anything new happening in the human system).

For an organism to evolve, it also requires recurrence; the continuation of the same things happening over and over again. For the people and the culture in an organization to evolve, the organization needs to adopt traditions, habits, and rituals that are part of the natural sequence of events – and they need to happen over and over again.

As a leader committed to catalyzing positive change in the organization, it is important to understand the time commitment it will require from yourself and anyone else involved in the change. In all our years of experience, as well as in the research we have done, we have seen that it takes just about 20% of the leaders' time to make positive, lasting change happen. This 20% includes functions such as visioning, planning, communicating, leading and empowering others to lead.

Chapter 15

Nurturing Humanistic Organizations to Achieve at Warp Speed

You've arrived at the final chapter in this guidebook and master class. In this chapter you'll learn how to achieve breakthrough performance in your organization. Just imagine a workplace where everyone is courageous, engaged, and innovative. When there's a problem, people most affected by it come together to solve it, regardless of job title or personal grievances. It's not about whose job it is or who offended who; it's about fixing the problem. This is a beacon of a healthy, strong organization we all want to work in. Often this type of culture is characterized as cohesive, collaborative, and innovative.

Remember that humanistic, along with achievement, affiliative, and self-actualization, are all required for an ideal culture; the type of environment where the above the line energy is palatable. All four elements are fundamental to generate the kind of culture where intrinsic motivation, exceptional teamwork and unrivaled innovation is a regular occurrence.

But what happens when there's a leak in the boat and someone needs to take responsibility? While it IS important to take ownership for bailing the water out of the boat, it is not about blaming anyone for the breakdown. It is about stopping the problem currently and in the future. When your human system is operating above the line, more often than not, you are able to handle the setback at warp speed. You've got people in courage, engagement, or innovation. However, when the human system is operating below the line, you would likely have the scenario embroiled in blaming and finger-pointing without a resolution or solution. Sometimes stepping on toes is inevitable in the process of fixing a problem. In such cases, it's important to apologize and make amends, but do not stop the momentum of progress. Ideally, engaged people taking on problems as a team and solving them for good is what we are aiming for.

A strong and thriving culture is the foundation of any successful organization. It is important to create an ideal vision of what a high-performance culture looks like. Make sure to include all four elements (Achievement, Self-Actualizing, Humanistic, and Affiliative) to ensure it is a healthy and intentional environment, as well as high performing.

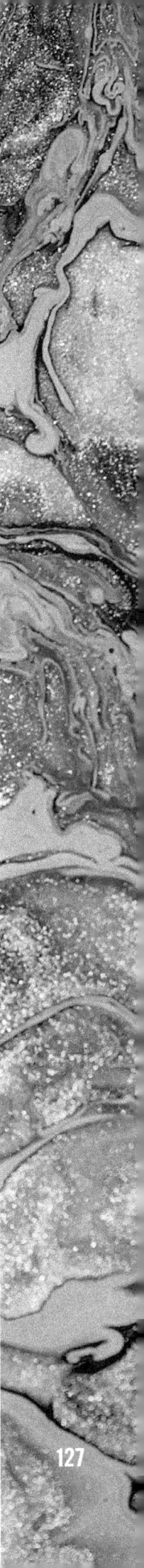

As you write your vision for your ideal culture, make sure to include details of what you will be seeing; how people will be acting, interacting, solving problems, taking on challenges, etc. Take time and really think this through.

Next, it is important to write out how you will avoid, or what you need to do to shift, any transactional, entangled, or toxic behavior that may be happening in the environment. Take a quick memorial tour of each department and each leader, and document any problematic behavior that could be constraining what is possible for your human system.

The Cycle of Organizational Transformation

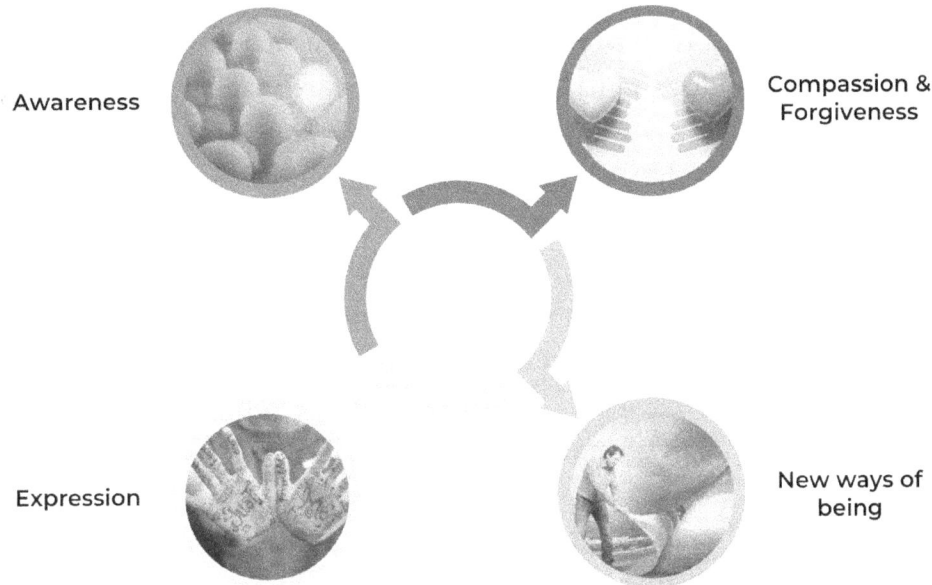

Awareness

Compassion & Forgiveness

Expression

New ways of being

Every organization and the people in them experience change differently. As you move forward, keep in mind that people have a past. They have reflections, projections, and feelings about what's happened and how it negatively or positively impacted them. The Cycle of Transformation is a cycle and it requires presence, patience, and vision to keep moving people forward.

As you know now, breakthrough performance is not a given; the environment has to be ripe for emergence. Organizational Culture is energy and energy has the power to create, to destroy or to stagnate.

Whether you are taking your organizational culture up a notch, or completely transforming how your human system interacts and works together – it all begins with a strong Vision for WHY. Why is it important to focus on this NOW?

Once you are clear what you want and why you want it, it is time to socialize it with a small group of people. Remember to enroll them in what is possible with this new type of emergent culture. Test the waters and gauge how people are responding to your communication. Once you have the small group feedback, it is time to make the bigger declaration of what you want to create. Follow the same guidance as we gave you with the small group. The only difference is now you will ask the small group to chime in on why they believe this is an important endeavor. After the declaration, announcement, and enrollment period, it is time to get into data collection mode. You will need support to gather the right data, in the right way, from the right people. Do your best to be inclusive and gain that infinite perspective we talked about previously. As you select and engage your support system, make sure you have a wide array of people on the Change Catalyst team. You will need a strong facilitator, and a few people who can be trained to be strong facilitators. Depending on the scale of this project, you will need one or more solid project managers, several really good listeners, as well as people who respect and enjoy analyzing data and looking for trends. If you have access to a coach and a trainer who has lead culture transformational programs, it will save you hundreds of hours of misguided time.

Achieving at warp speed requires a commitment to creating a strong and thriving culture. You are strongly encouraged to prioritize the ongoing journey of personal and cultural transformation and to be intentional and mindful about the changes you want to see in your organization. Slowing down to make a plan brings warp speed much more readily than the adrenaline bias of your earlier days. This involves taking the first step by starting to have conversations with your team and really listening and then identifying partners who can support you on your journey.

We trust this chapter has been helpful in providing you with the tools and knowledge you need to ignite your organization's culture.

The foundation of healthy, intentional & high-performance organizational culture is trust. Thank you for trusting us and participating in the *Ignite Culture* train the trainer guidebook and Masterclass. Remember we are here to support you along your journey.

Key Takeaways

- If you slow down and have a plan, you can achieve high performance more quickly.

- Take the time to transform yourself, your executive team, and your culture. Do the work that is required. The investment comes back tenfold.

- Trust is a catalyst that, at its highest level, ignites synchronicity and emergent behavior, which, in turn, unleashes exponential human potential.

- Remember: Go slow to go *fast*.

What is your biggest takeaway from this book?

What should you do first?

Where do you need support?

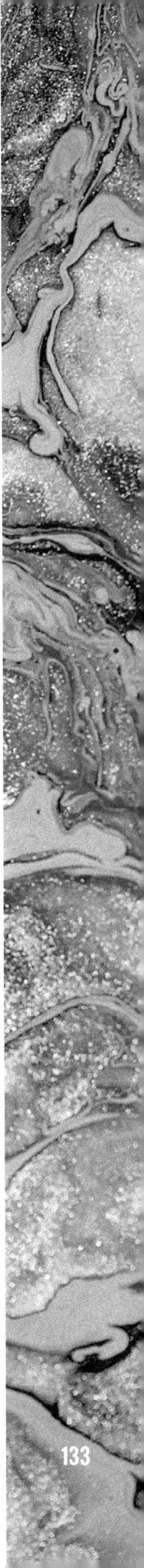

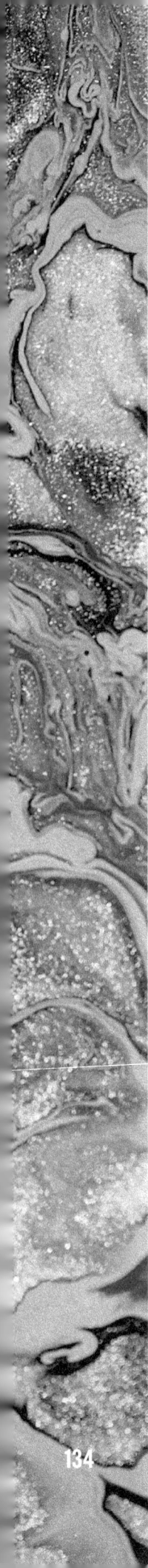